CAMBRIDGE LIBRARY COLLECTION

Books of enduring scholarly value

Egyptology

The large–scale scientific investigation of Egyptian antiquities by Western scholars began as an unintended consequence of Napoleon's invasion of Egypt during which, in 1799, the Rosetta Stone was discovered. The military expedition was accompanied by French scholars, whose reports prompted a wave of enthusiasm that swept across Europe and North America resulting in the Egyptian Revival style in art and architecture. Increasing numbers of tourists visited Egypt, eager to see the marvels being revealed by archaeological excavation. Writers and booksellers responded to this growing interest with publications ranging from technical site reports to tourist guidebooks and from children's histories to theories identifying the pyramids as repositories of esoteric knowledge. This series reissues a wide selection of such books. They reveal the gradual change from the 'tomb-robbing' approach of early excavators to the highly organised and systematic approach of Flinders Petrie, the 'father of Egyptology', and include early accounts of the decipherment of the hieroglyphic script.

A Wayfarer in Egypt

The Egyptologist Annie Quibell, née Pirie (1862–1927) originally trained as an artist, but became a student of Sir Flinders Petrie, copying wall-paintings and inscriptions at his Saqqara excavations, where she met her husband, who was an inspector for the Egyptian Antiquities Service. Accompanying him and sharing in his work on site, she was keen to popularise the marvels of ancient Egyptian civilisation, recreating life-sized Egyptian rooms for a display at the St Louis World's Fair in 1904, and writing several works for the lay reader. This book, published in 1925, is intended to 'point out to other sojourners and travellers some things about Egypt, which, after long residence there, seem to me important'. As well as discussing the famous archaeological sites, Quibell de⸻ Port Said (the entrance to the Suez Canal), and the Nile delta, the ⸻ and an expedition into the desert.

Cambridge University Press has long been a pioneer in the reissuing of out-of-print titles from its own backlist, producing digital reprints of books that are still sought after by scholars and students but could not be reprinted economically using traditional technology. The Cambridge Library Collection extends this activity to a wider range of books which are still of importance to researchers and professionals, either for the source material they contain, or as landmarks in the history of their academic discipline.

Drawing from the world-renowned collections in the Cambridge University Library and other partner libraries, and guided by the advice of experts in each subject area, Cambridge University Press is using state-of-the-art scanning machines in its own Printing House to capture the content of each book selected for inclusion. The files are processed to give a consistently clear, crisp image, and the books finished to the high quality standard for which the Press is recognised around the world. The latest print-on-demand technology ensures that the books will remain available indefinitely, and that orders for single or multiple copies can quickly be supplied.

The Cambridge Library Collection brings back to life books of enduring scholarly value (including out-of-copyright works originally issued by other publishers) across a wide range of disciplines in the humanities and social sciences and in science and technology.

A Wayfarer in Egypt

ANNIE ABERNETHIE PIRIE QUIBELL

CAMBRIDGE
UNIVERSITY PRESS

CAMBRIDGE
UNIVERSITY PRESS

University Printing House, Cambridge, CB2 8BS, United Kingdom

Cambridge University Press is part of the University of Cambridge.
It furthers the University's mission by disseminating knowledge in the pursuit of
education, learning and research at the highest international levels of excellence.

www.cambridge.org
Information on this title: www.cambridge.org/9781108081955

© in this compilation Cambridge University Press 2017

This edition first published 1925
This digitally printed version 2017

ISBN 978-1-108-08195-5 Paperback

A WAYFARER IN EGYPT

HEAD OF QUEEN NEFERTITI

[*Frontispiece*

A WAYFARER IN EGYPT

BY

ANNIE A. QUIBELL

WITH SIXTEEN ILLUSTRATIONS AND A MAP

METHUEN & CO. LTD.
36 ESSEX STREET W.C
LONDON

First published in 1925

PRINTED IN GREAT BRITAIN

PREFACE

CHILDREN of the West, we are all wayfarers and strangers in an Eastern land, and can only grope uncertainly after the realities around us.

All that is aimed at in this book is that it may point out to other sojourners and travellers some things about Egypt, which, after long residence there, seem to me important. To this end, a goodly portion of the vast bulk of literature on the subject has been consulted, but of more value to me than many books has been the privilege of close and friendly association with most of the scholars and archæologists through whose exertions during the last quarter of a century so much has been revealed to the world. For their help and guidance, for the ideals they set forth of patient labour and balanced judgment, I can never be sufficiently grateful.

I am indebted to many of these friends for the beautiful photographs which I have been permitted to publish, and would specially wish to express my thanks to Mr. H. Burton and the Trustees of the Metropolitan Museum of New York, to Capt. Creswell, to Mr. Tottenham, late Director-General of the Public Works Department of Egypt, to Mr. Watt of the Assuan Dam, to Mr. Cairns of the Survey of Egypt, to the authorities of the Berlin Museum, and lastly and chiefly, to Mr. C. M. Firth, Mr. J. E. Quibell and the officials of the Service des Antiquités, Cairo.

ANNIE A. QUIBELL

September, 1925.

CONTENTS

LIST OF ILLUSTRATIONS

ix

BOOKS RECOMMENDED

HANDBOOKS

Guide to Alexandria	Forster
Alexandrea ad Ægyptum . . .	Breccia
Rambles in Cairo	Mrs. Devonshire
Some Cairo Mosques	,, ,,
Quatrevingts mosquées et autres monuments musulmanes . . .	,, ,,
Egyptian History and Art (with special reference to Museum collections) .	Mrs. A. A. Quibell
Tombs of Sakkara	,, ,, ,,
Pyramids of Giza	,, ,, ,,
Guide to the Antiquities of Upper Egypt	Weigall

HISTORY

History of Egypt	Breasted
Egyptian religion	,,
Life in Ancient Egypt . . .	Erman
Empire of the Ptolemies . . .	Mahaffy
Arab Conquest of Egypt . . .	Butler
History of Egypt (Saracen period) .	Stanley Lane Poole
Cairo (Medieval Towns series) . .	,, ,, ,,
Egypt in the Nineteenth Century .	Cameron
England in Egypt	Milner

TRAVELS, ETC.

Manners and Customs of the Modern Egyptians	Lane
Letters from Egypt	Lady Duff Gordon
Children of the Nile	Marmaduke Pickthall
Harems et Musulmanes . . .	Niya Salima
Tutankhamon, Vol. I	Carter and Mace
Problem of the Obelisks . . .	Engelbach

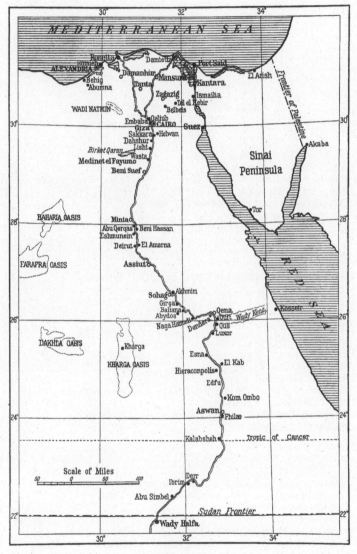

MAP OF EGYPT

A WAYFARER IN EGYPT

CHAPTER I

ALEXANDRIA

ONCE upon a time the crews and passengers and toiling slaves that had crossed the Mediterranean in tall ships and long galleys, saw, flashing high above the low African coast, the beams from the first great lighthouse in the world, and by day, as they drew near to Alexandria, there rose upon their vision a prospect of walls and towers and palaces gleaming white and splendid above the blue water, and their hearts rejoiced to see such an ending to their weary voyage. Where is all this splendour to-day?

The wayfarer of the twentieth century, crossing in a comfortable ferry boat, sees a row of unimposing buildings breaking but a very little the flat coast line, and gradually distinguishes the breakwaters, docks and shipping in the fine harbour, but singularly little of the town behind. Alexandria of the past, founded by a hero of romance, the intellectual capital of the world under his Greek successors, the setting for the loves of Antony and Cleopatra, the great religious centre in the early days of Christianity, has vanished as if it had never been. All that remains is its climate, its blue sea and its excellent situation as a port and gathering-place for all the commerce of the Levant.

As the steamer warps its way into harbour one small boat after another puts out to meet it, decked with the flags of every hotel in Cairo and Alexandria ; amid a babel of noise and the distant waving of handkerchiefs and hats from the crowded quay. If one is arriving in the East for the first

1

time, it is rather lively and amusing, but amusement is soon
merged in unpleasant excitement when the rush of porters
and hotel touts comes on board, and most people, tired and
bewildered with the din and the fighting with wild beasts to
get their luggage through the Customs, are thankful to subside
into the peace of a comfortable hotel, or better still, to catch
the train to Cairo and get done with it. So Alexandria is
only thought of as a port to land at or leave from and hardly
counts as part of Egypt. Indeed, with only a short time to
dispose of, it is best to treat it so, for other things are much
more interesting and much more strange.

But there are people who come to Alexandria and Alexandria
only, for business reasons, and there are others who come to
Egypt for a long winter and stay late into the spring, and
such may find that Alexandria has more to offer than appears
at first sight. In the early summer when Cairo is hot and
dusty, there is a different climate down here ; a cool breeze,
a sparkling sea, gardens fresh and blooming and beautiful
bathing. Because the seaside is so much more attractive than
inland the town has extended east and west for a long way, to
Mex and Ramleh. The western part has unfortunately grown
into a very mean quarter, which prevents Mex from ever
becoming popular, though once you get there it is a pleasant
spot enough, but the eastern suburb is a much frequented
watering-place and runs out for many miles along the shore,
narrow, like a stretched string, on which the stations of the
electric tramway form a line of knots.

The present town of Alexandria was mostly built by
Mehemet Aly, the great-grandfather of the reigning king of
Egypt. He ruled Egypt from 1809 till 1848 and did his best
to give it the outward appearance of a progressive and civilized
state. Before he raised himself to power, Alexandria had
dwindled to insignificance, for during the Middle Ages the
Canopic mouth of the Nile had dried up and Alexandria could
no longer attract much trade, there being no waterway into
the country. Rosetta, at the mouth of the Bolbitine branch,
took its place as the principal port of Egypt. But Rosetta,
on its sandy beach, could never become a good harbour and

Mehemet Aly saw how much the country would gain by reverting to Alexandria, so, as soon as he could afford it, he set about the construction of a canal which should connect the port with the Nile a considerable distance inland. Directly this canal was made, Alexandria began to flourish again and Rosetta to decline.

The change it brought about is well realized in reading two books of travel, one written early in Mehemet Aly's reign, the other near its end. The first is by Belzoni, who went to Egypt in 1815, with his wife, and describes their landing in the month of May at Alexandria, where they found the plague raging and were quarantined for several weeks in what he calls the French Occale, under hideously uncomfortable conditions. When the plague subsided, towards the end of June, they hired a boat which put to sea, but was driven back by bad weather ; however, on the following day they got round to Rosetta and sailed up the Nile in four days from there to Boulac, the port of Cairo.

Belzoni's accounts of the country are especially valuable, because he and his wife were not rich people and could get none of the favour and protection which, even then, were available for well-to-do and influential travellers. His description of the absolutely mediæval conditions prevailing in Cairo and in Egypt generally, are in striking contrast with what Miss Martineau, writing thirty years later, has to say. She was perhaps, after Herodotus, the most intelligent tourist who ever wrote a book on Egypt. Her landing was in 1846, in November, and she and her party spent four days in Alexandria, where they " enjoyed the hospitality of several European residents." There seems to have been a good hotel, where the passengers to India by the overland route spent a night or two on their way out or home. An hotel omnibus took Miss Martineau and her friends to the Mahmoudieh Canal, where they found a steamer waiting and only took a day and a half to reach Boulac.

I quote her statements about the making of the canal, as they are very interesting, and, I believe thoroughly well founded.

" This is the canal which, as everybody knows, cost the lives of above twenty thousand people, from the Pasha's hurry to have it finished, and the want of due preparation for such a work in such a country. Without tools and sufficient food, the poor creatures brought here by compulsion to work, died off rapidly under fatigue and famine. Before the improvements of the Pasha are vaunted in European periodicals as putting European enterprises to shame, it might be as well to ascertain their cost,—in other things as well as money ;— the taxes of pain and death, as well as of piastres, which are levied to pay the Pasha's public work. There must be some ground for the horror which impels a whole population to such practices as are every day seen in Egypt to keep out of the reach of Government :—practices such as putting out an eye, pulling out the teeth necessary for biting cartridges and cutting off a forefinger, to incapacitate men for army service. . . . Any misfortune is to be encountered rather than that of entering the Pasha's army, the Pasha's manufactories, the Pasha's schools. This can hardly be all baseless folly on the part of the people. If questioned, they could point, at least, to the twenty-three thousand deaths which took place in six months in the making of the Mahmoudieh canal."

The railway from Alexandria was made very early—in 1855—but the canal is still very much used for slow traffic.

Mehemet Aly laid out the town on a rather spacious scale, and the large square which bears his name and has his statue in the middle, is a handsome centre for the city. But Alexandria suffered terribly in the bombardment—or rather, in the riots that followed the bombardment—of 1882 and the parts that have been rebuilt are unprepossessing. This comparatively modern history is becoming so hazy in many minds that perhaps a page or two giving a brief summary of it will not come amiss.

Mehemet Aly's government was extremely oppressive to the Egyptians, but favoured foreign settlers and, on the whole, the country prospered greatly under him and his successors, until, in 1863, his grandson Ismail became Khedive. Ismail was inordinately vain. He had all the instincts and desires of an Oriental despot, but posed as an enlightened western ruler; wishing really to take his place among European potentates as a kind of modern Haroun el Raschid or Soliman the Magnificent, and all in the best Paris style. Inevitably he soon wanted to borrow, and, Egypt being even then very rich, he borrowed at first on easy terms and felt sure that he had unlimited sources of wealth behind him. But he was surrounded by a set of unscrupulous financiers who made fortunes themselves, but saw to it that less and less from each loan went to the Khedive. Had it not been for the American War, and the immensely increased price of cotton which resulted from it, the crash would have come sooner than it did, but even so, in 1869, when Ismail dazzled Europe by his magnificence on the occasion of the opening of the Suez Canal, he was well on the way to be the bankrupt ruler of a bankrupt state. In 1875 Lord Beaconsfield bought his large holding of Canal shares for England, which have turned out to be a very brilliant investment. A year or two later and the game was up. No more loans could be raised, for nothing more wherewith to pay interest could be wrung out of the Egyptian peasantry, and not only was a state of famine becoming normal, but nothing had been done for years to keep up the irrigation works on which the life of Egypt depends. The bondholders were largely French, but there were many English as well, and after some negotiations, English and French Commissioners were appointed as liquidators and set apart the revenues of Ismail's private estates to pay the interest, but saw clearly that little could be done so long as Ismail, who was notoriously keeping very bad faith, remained at the head of affairs.

The next step was what is known as the Dual Control, whereby England and France jointly took charge of the finances, and they managed to have Ismail deposed and his son Tewfik appointed in his place. Tewfik was a very different man from his father, and a far more honest one, but his position was very difficult. The Dual Control had no means of enforcing their reforms and the troubles of Egypt needed more drastic treatment than the mere remodelling of the finance could give; moreover, a Dual Control is not very

2

likely to be a success in public any more than in private con-
cerns. Tewfik, surrounded by Turkish intrigues and very
conscious of the wretched state of Egypt, did not know whom
he could trust. Things went from bad to worse, until, in
the beginning of 1881, the Egyptian officers of the army, who
had been shockingly ill-treated, gave voice to their grievances
under the leadership of Colonel Ahmed Arabi ; one of their
chief complaints being that they were excluded from any of
the higher commands, which were all given to Turks. Nothing
was done, either to subdue the disaffection or to redress the
wrongs ; mutiny followed and flourished, until the Khedive
was dominated by Arabi and compelled to accept his terms.
England had, long before, along with several other European
powers, pledged herself to maintain the dynasty of Mehemet
Aly in Egypt ; France was not one of the contracting powers,
but had been by far the strongest influence in Egypt throughout the nineteenth century, and it was England and France
together who were now endeavouring to work out the financial
reforms. But who could have foreseen such a hopeless situation ? The leader of the mutineers now Minister of War, the
Treasury empty, creditors clamorous, the country destitute,
and, to add to the difficulties, storm clouds beginning to gather
in the Sudan. Looking back over nearly half a century, one
can see that there was some case for leaving the whole thing
alone, as the French did. They withdrew, but England felt
that her honour was too much involved. Egypt had once
been prosperous and law abiding ; with some help she might
be so again : besides, though England had never wanted the
Suez Canal, now that it was there, it was of supreme importance to keep some hold upon it. But there were divided
counsels for a while, and Admiral Seymour, who commanded
the fleet that was watching proceedings at Alexandria, must
often have been in doubt as to what he was expected to do.
A riot broke out in Alexandria in June, 1882, in which a good
many Europeans lost their lives and the large commercial
community was thrown into panic. Some people believe
that Arabi had a hand in fomenting this disturbance, in order
to make it clear that his was the only authority capable of

dealing with it ; anyhow, when he was appealed to, he promptly brought troops and restored order. So far, well ; but after this he appeared to be taking steps to constitute himself dictator, and in particular, to be preparing to defy England. He began building forts round the town, which could only be intended as a menace to the British Fleet. Admiral Seymour ordered him to stop, warning Arabi that, if he continued, the forts would be demolished. Arabi took no notice, went on building, and on July 11 the Admiral ordered the bombardment. This did a great deal of damage to the forts, and by that evening Arabi had evacuated the place and retired several miles inland. But, as Admiral Seymour did not follow up his action by occupying the town, which had been left with no military or police force, an appalling riot ensued ; whole quarters of Alexandria were laid in ruins and the entire industrial and commercial system collapsed.

The subsequent history of the events of 1882 will be better told in the following chapter, in which the route from Port Said to Cairo goes over the ground of Arabi's final overthrow. In Alexandria things righted gradually, but the place must have lost most of the Oriental character it formerly had.

It is extremely difficult, even with a map of Alexandria before us, to understand what the town looked like in ancient days, for its configuration has totally changed and some parts of the Ptolemaic city are now below sea-level, while parts which were once under water are now dry land. In old times the Eastern harbour was the one most used ; now all the shipping comes and goes from the Western harbour. The two are separated by a peninsula of very recent formation. The hammer head of this peninsula is the island of Pharos, which lies east and west. The great lighthouse was at its eastern extremity, where the ruins of Kait Bey's fort now stand : many of the fine squared blocks that belonged to the lighthouse can be seen round about. It was 500 feet in height and four-storied ; the lowest story, 200 feet high, contained the acommodation for the keepers and mechanics as well as storehouses for fuel and implements. The second story was octagonal, the third circular and at the top was the lantern, which must have been covered by some sort of dome. A huge bonfire blazed here nightly, but there was also a mirror, which was very celebrated, and functioned by day, but I do not think its use has ever been satisfactorily explained. A long causeway, the Heptastadion, connected the island with the town and was pierced by several openings to admit of boats passing from the one harbour to the other. As the town fell into decay, this causeway silted up and buildings rose upon the rubbish, gradually extending it until, in late Arab times, most of the population were gathered there, thus converting the Pharos from an island into the peninsula of the present day. The big square laid out by Mehemet Aly, with his statue in the middle of it, is built upon this neck of land reclaimed from the sea. In an open space not far from it, now the terminus of the Ramleh trams, once stood the two obelisks known as Cleopatra's Needles, although they never had anything to do with her. Nearly fifteen hundred years before the shape of her fascinating nose set the world in jeopardy, Thothmes III had erected these obelisks in the Temple of Heliopolis ; the Romans brought them to Alexandria when they were ruling the country, a little after Cleopatra's time, and there they remained, all through the Middle Ages, great landmarks from sea and shore, till the nineteenth century, when they were moved again, and farther afield, for one of them is now in Central Park, New York, and the other on the Thames Embankment.

A little farther to the east, a promontory, where once the Ptolemaic palace stood, juts out into the harbour. The University, Museum and Library were somewhere near by and probably connected with the royal palace, but all trace of these buildings has disappeared. The most famous temple of Alexandria, the Serapeum, was on higher ground, a little distance inland, and some evidence of its former glory is still to be seen, though almost the only thing that remains above ground is the so-called Pompey's pillar. It had no more to do with Pompey than Cleopatra's Needles had with Cleopatra ;

in fact it is a later piece of work altogether and was probably set up in the Serapeum in honour of the Emperor Diocletian, in the third century A.D. But in the enclosure surrounding it are long subterranean galleries which must have belonged to the Temple.

Two groups of ancient tombs are worth a visit. Of these, Kom el Shugafa, near Pompey's pillar, is the larger and perhaps the more important. It is a sort of Catacomb, three stories deep, the lowest being under water. The whole tomb, stairs, chambers and galleries, has been hewn out of the rock and is rather impressive, in spite of the hybrid, queer vulgarity of its decoration. The date is of the second century A.D., after the Roman Occupation of Egypt was well established.

The other catacombs at Anfouchy, on the Pharos, are smaller, older and rather better in style. They are of the late Ptolemaic period, with Roman additions. A few other tombs have been found here and there about the town, in the digging of foundations and laying of water pipes to modern houses, but the ancient streets and the Ptolemaic drainage system are too far below the present water-level to permit of any thorough excavation being made.

The small objects found on the Alexandrian sites are housed in the Museum, a collection which has been made the most of by an admirable curator, Professor Breccia, and is of considerable interest to scholars, but rather depressing to the ordinary visitor. The Egyptian things in it may be skipped with a good conscience ; there are so many and so much better in Cairo, but there are some good Greek objects ; a few fragments of really high-class sculpture and one or two fine heads of Serapis, interesting, as showing how entirely Greek he is in origin, and how closely he is approximated in art to the type of Zeus. Of small sculpture, some little terracotta figurines are charming ; they are like Tanagra statuettes, but have a character of their own. And there is a fine collection of Ptolemaic coins. The ancient Egyptians did not coin money, but after they had begun to trade extensively with the Greeks, they used the little silver Athenian owl, which was current round most of the Mediterranean, and, after

Ptolemy I there is a complete and beautiful series of Egyptian coins.

Not much remains from the Christian churches of Alexandria, but there is a superb capital, which probably came from one of the four columns which supported the dome of the Cathedral of St. Mark. No one knows when this great church fell into ruins. The Arab conquerors do not seem to have deliberately destroyed it, but they could not be expected to keep it in repair. We may reasonably suppose, however, that it was still standing when the Venetians carried off the body of the saint in a basket, slung between two trusty men who held their noses and called out " pig " to discourage the Muslims at the Alexandria Customs, as they have been at pains to tell us on the mosaics in San Marco. Certainly it seems to have been a most justifiable, not to say laudable, theft, for nobody missed him out of Alexandria, while the Venetians gloried and still rejoice in the possession of the relic.

But there is little in the Museum or in the town that can bring the ancient Alexandria to life again for us. A better way to take in something of its extent and grandeur is to go out of it. An excursion along the east coast will show us Abukir and Canopus, and, out to the west, beyond Lake Mariout, is a most interesting bit of country, closely connected with the old Alexandrian history.

Abukir is the easier trip to manage, as it makes a pleasant motor drive out past Ramleh, with its hotels and bathing beaches and big new houses. Abukir was the scene of a good many events during the Napoleonic Expedition to Egypt, the chief one being the Battle of the Nile, in 1798. Napoleon's fleet had managed to elude Nelson's pursuit and Napoleon, as soon as he landed, had made a dash off for Cairo with the troops, leaving Admiral Brueys in command of the fleet, with instructions to dispose of the ships with the utmost regard to safety from attack. Admiral Brueys sailed round to the Bay of Abukir, believing it to be a perfectly safe anchorage. Nelson, by a brilliant manœuvre, got half his fleet round into the Bay, behind the French fleet, and attacked at the same time from the open sea with the other half. The French fleet was completely destroyed and Napoleon was thereby left locked up in Egypt with his army. A year later there was a battle on land with a different result. Turkey had by that time declared war on France and landed an army of 15,000 men at Abukir with the intention of occupying Egypt and dislodging the French. Napoleon hurried down from Cairo with Kléber and Murat, engaged the Turks and drove nearly the whole force into the sea. This battle had a great importance for the subsequent history of Egypt, for this is the first occasion when Mehemet Aly comes upon the scene. He was Albanian by race, a native of Kavalla, and was serving as an officer of Bashi Bazouks with the Turkish army. He was among the many soldiers driven into the sea by the French, but was rescued by a boat from Sir Sydney Smith's fleet, which was watching the course of the battle. He reappears, fighting with the allied British and Turkish army in the next expedition, that under Sir Ralph Abercrombie, which landed in 1801, again with the object of driving out the French. Sir Ralph Abercrombie died of wounds after an action between Abukir and Ramleh, but the expedition was successful on the whole, for the French army evacuated Egypt and were allowed to retire with the honours of war. Mehemet Aly stayed on and gradually raised himself to power on the ruins of the Mamelukes. If he had not been fished out of the water by the English sailors, how different all the history of the nineteenth century might have been !

Close to Abukir, on a high bluff, stand the ruins, or rather, the site of Canopus. Very little remains to show that it was once a large watering-place with a fine temple to Serapis, a bath establishment and many country houses, but further excavations on the site may be productive of better results. A good many things have been found there, the most important being an inscribed slab, now in Cairo Museum, which was very useful in the decipherment of the old Egyptian language. Like the Rosetta stone, the Canopic inscription was in three languages, or, more correctly, in two languages and three scripts, hieroglyphic, demotic and Greek. The Rosetta stone, which was deciphered some thirty years earlier, gave the real clue

to the ancient language, but the Canopic stone was a most
satisfactory confirmation for the scholars, as their translation
of the Egyptian text was in complete agreement with the
Greek version.

Farther along the coast eastwards is Rosetta, which can
now be reached by motor-car. It was, as we have seen, the
port which flourished in the late Middle Ages, when Alexandria
had declined, owing to the drying up of the Canopic mouth
of the Nile. After the opening of the Mahmoudieh Canal,
when trade reverted to Alexandria, Rosetta gradually stag-
nated, and for this reason it has not been much altered or
rebuilt, so that, like Damietta,which has had a similar history,
it remains as it was in the seventeenth and eighteenth centuries ; a little Turkish town with a curious architecture,
decidedly worth seeing for anyone interested in the period.

But by far the most attractive excursion from Alexandria is
westwards into the coastlands of the Libyan desert. There
is a railway, and one can make a good day in early spring
when the wild flowers are in bloom, by taking train to Behig
or Amria and wandering about towards the seaside. It is
the only place in Egypt where there are wild flowers, but here,
for a brief season in February or early March, the wilderness
literally breaks forth into blossom. But if one wants to see
more—and there is a good deal to see—it is necessary to go
by car, or better still, to make a short camping trip. A
motor can go almost everywhere, and I have spent a very
delightful day in that way, but it is a little fatiguing.

After Mex, when for two or three miles the road goes
through limestone quarries, the surface is appallingly bad, but
beyond that the going is very fair. Once past the quarries,
we cross a dyke over the end of Lake Mariout, and then have,
the open desert ahead. There are tracks of camels, goats
and even of motor-cars, but one is not tied down to follow
them closely, for in many parts the car can run where it likes,
only it is well to have a good map, or a chauffeur who knows
his directions. It is desert, yet not the typical desert, for
there is a rainfall, and it must be remembered that this is
the beginning of the North African belt that was one of the

granaries of Rome. There is a barley crop grown now, but
it is only every third year or so that it is worth much ; as
I saw it one May, the rain had failed and the scanty stalks were
not worth the reaping. The glory of the flowers was past, and
there was little to see but a small mesembryanthemum and the
brown stems of asphodel.

I do not know whether the rainfall is less now than in Roman
times, but it never can have been abundant, for as we go
farther west there are many signs of the painstaking ancient
cultivation ; rock cisterns to collect the water flowing down
from the higher ground, and careful utilization of the subterranean streams which are to be found near the sea. It is
very curious to see gardens enclosed by walls, much silted up
with sand, but still, with vines and fig trees flourishing,
nourished by the subsoil waters. No labourer's cottage stands
among them; they are cared for by the Bedouᵢn of the surrounding desert.

Near the station of Behig, a new and very picturesque
town has grown up since the War, partly owing to industries
which were developed among the Arab women, who had been
reduced to starvation by Senussi raids and had to be supported
by the Egyptian Government. The management of the
subsidy was entrusted to Miss Nina Baird, an artist and an
Arabic scholar, who, acting on the principle that the assistance
ought to be given in wages and not in doles, set the women
on to the work that they were able to do. They weave the
hair of their goats into the material for their own black tents
on queer little flat looms, and, under Miss Baird's direction,
they began to make rugs and carpets of very pleasing design
and colour, which found a ready sale in Cairo and Alexandria.
Lines upon lines of the black tents surround this new settlement of Burg, and, thanks to the artistic genius and resource-
fulness of Colonel Bramly of the Frontier Districts Administration, the buildings of this city in the wilderness are extraordinarily imposing and well suited to the lonely desert round
about. There are sad changes already, for Miss Baird died
in the early days of her enterprise, Colonel Bramly has retired
from the Egyptian service and the Government have dis-

continued the carpet factory. It is much to be hoped that
all their work will not be completely lost, but the outlook is
not encouraging.

This settlement of Burg is not far from Behig station and
could be visited on foot, but the Monastery of Abumna, or
Abu Menas, lies several miles away to the south and to get
there, a motor or a tent is absolutely necessary.

There must have been some change in the climatic conditions
or in the configuration of the country since this was an inhabited monastery. The Community could not have existed
so far from water as Abu Menas now is. Although the reflec-
tion may arise in the ribald mind that the monks probably
did not wash much and may have drunk wine, that does not
meet the case, for not only was there a monastery, but also
a bath establishment. The baths are still to be seen : large
concreted Roman baths, and, besides that, the hosts of pilgrims
to the site all took away with them little flasks of water with a
figure of the saint between two camels stamped upon them.
These " Menas " bottles are well known in museums. The
reason for the saint and the camels is that Menas was a
Roman officer and a Christian, who belonged to Alexandria,
but was martyred in Asia Minor. His comrades brought his
ashes back to Egypt and laid them on a camel, which marched
off with them into the Libyan desert and on and on till at
length it lay down, signifying that on that spot the remains
of the saint were to be buried. But it is said that the place
was forgotten after that, until miracles of healing began to
occur there : a shepherd noticed that a sick sheep which
passed over the grave was promptly cured and he tried another
sheep with the same success. Then, somehow, it began to
get a name ; a princess was miraculously restored to health
and its fame became established.

A marvellous group of buildings gathered round the tomb,
a splendid church, lined with varied and costly marbles, a
hospice for the pilgrims, baths, bakeries, stables, in short, a
regular monastic town. There is a huge well built of fine
masonry, but now blocked up with stones. One wonders
whether water would still be found at the bottom, if the

expense of digging it out could be undertaken. The Monastery was excavated a few years before the War by a German savant, the Abbé Kauffmann. Although in a ruinous state, there is quite enough left to show its great extent and the magnificence of some of the buildings. The church is interesting to students of Christian architecture, as it may fairly be said to be pre-Byzantine, all the earliest and best fragments being more or less " classical " in style. Beyond, and all around, as far as the eye can reach, is nothing but waterless desert. No one knows when the water dried up and the holy site was abandoned. It could not have flourished after the Mohammedan conquest, though in so remote a spot it would probably be left alone ; indeed, as I read in Mr. Forster's admirable " Guide to Alexandria," as late as A.D. 1000 an Arab traveller saw the great double basilica still standing. Lights burned in the shrine by night and day, and there was still left a little trickle of the " beautiful water of St. Menas that drives away pain."

In the other direction from Behig station, down by the seaside, are remarkable remains of an older period. In Ptolemaic times the wealthy Alexandrians had villas and country houses all along this bit of coast, and exceedingly agreeable summer residences they must have been, for the seashore hereabouts has a singular charm ; the air is pure and strong, the beach is glittering white ; being formed of minute grains of limestone (oolites), while the colour of the sea, looking through to this white floor, is the most brilliant and translucent blue it is possible to imagine.

Ptolemaic and Roman ruins are to be found anywhere in this district. On the sea side, not far from Behig, there was once a large town, Taposiris Magna, with a harbour and a lighthouse, one of a chain of beacon lights that is said to have stretched all the way from Alexandria to Cyrene. This one is now known as Abusir, a common Arabic place name, but in this case, evidently a corruption of the ancient Taposiris. A good part of this lighthouse is still standing, and, as it appears to have been built on the model of the Pharos, indeed to have been a kind of copy of it in miniature, it is of considerable importance. There is also the enclosure wall of a temple of Osiris, on a long ridge overlooking the sea ; a place of imposing size and very finely situated, but nothing is left of the temple buildings.

On the whole, thinking back over all that we saw on that wonderful day, the picture that rises in my mind more than the temple, the lighthouse, or even the lonely Monastery, is the landscape ; the austere, monotonous beauty of the desert, pale in the sunlight, the brown flocks, the white-clad shepherds and the long lines of the low black tents dotted over the wide expanse.

CHAPTER II

PORT SAID AND THE DELTA

THE low, flat coast of Africa becomes lower and flatter as it tails off towards the north-east, until sea and land intermingle and, at length, only a spit of land divides the salt marshes of Lake Menzaleh from the shallow shores of the Mediterranean. Then the deep trench of the Suez Canal cuts through the sandbanks and the marshes and runs southwards across the desert. On the edge of it, between Menzaleh and the sea, Port Said rises out of the watery waste. It was born of the Canal, grew with the Canal and lives by the Canal. A long pier runs out to sea and on the pier there stands the statue of Ferdinand de Lesseps, the creator of the Canal and of Port Said ; like a local god, welcoming the strangers who seek his domains. Let us keep for a little the image of the local deity and translate it as the Genius of the place. It was, and is, the French Genius. De Lesseps, with all his faults and mistakes, was a very patriotic Frenchman. It was for the glory of France that he carried through the Canal, and the French impress that he gave to it was stamped so strongly that French it remains, although it has been an international highway for more than half a century.

It did not suit England particularly well that the Canal should be made ; at least, it was Palmerston's belief that we were better without it, for he did not want to be involved in the Egyptian question more than he could possibly help. Since Napoleon's expedition there had always been an Egyptian question, and during the long reign of Mehemet Aly, it had several times caused serious friction among the European Powers. The opening of the Overland route to India, which

17

crossed from Alexandria to Suez, had speeded up the transmission of mails by many weeks and was available for the transport of troops in any great emergency, so it is intelligible enough that Palmerston was unable to see that any benefit would result to England from the construction of the Canal, to compensate for the undoubted difficulties in which it would involve her. Besides that, Palmerston and many of his advisers did not think it would be a success. When the Canal was designed, it was intended mainly for sailing vessels, and, as I read, it was the invention of the compound engine for steamers and the extraordinary development of our mercantile marine during the years that the Canal was under construction, that converted it from the " stagnant ditch " that Palmerston prophesied, into the great commercial highway of the world.

Mehemet Aly was interested and favourable to the scheme, but De Lesseps was unable to get a concession for it either from him or from his successor Abbas, and it was only after Said Pasha became Khedive in 1854 that the concession was granted and the work begun.

Said Pasha was the first of the Egyptian rulers to invite foreign interference with the finance and general management of the country. When he succeeded there was a revenue of about three millions and no debt, but he embarked on the policy of borrowing from Europe, which his nephew Ismail afterwards carried to such disastrous lengths. De Lesseps drew flattering pictures to the Pasha of the fame and credit that would accrue to him from the carrying out of such a magnificent work, but, as a matter of fact, there was nothing but outlay for Egypt, with no recompense save in the remote future.

Egypt really renounced a good deal, when, besides losing the considerable amount of profit she derived from the traffic going by the Overland route, she agreed to forgo all dues collected by the Canal, in favour of the Company, and also to provide most of the labour required in the construction. By the terms of the contract, the Canal becomes the property of Egypt after 99 years from its opening ; that is to say, in

1968. It would be a bold prophet that would venture to predict what it may be worth then.

Port Said has grown and improved with the prosperity of the Canal, but it can never be anything but a rather dreary little place, with a good summer climate. The only interest about it is to watch the great ships that pass daily by on their voyages to and from the uttermost parts of the earth. To eastward the view is over salty desert ; to the west is the expanse of Lake Menzaleh. It is possible to cross the lake by a cargo boat to Damietta, or to Mataria, near Mansura, and so pass by some of the island mounds which mark the site of ancient towns. Menzaleh is a recently formed lake and these old towns stood once on fertile land, watered by three of the Nile branches ; now all dried up. Sometimes the bird life on this tract of brackish water is wonderful to watch ; this, of course, depends on the season.

Leaving Port Said by railway, the first stop is Kantara, which means " the Bridge," and, though except for a few years during the War there has never been an actual bridge there, in a wider sense, it is a real Bridge between Asia and Africa. This was the point where caravans coming across the Sinai Peninsula used to enter Egypt, and it is the way to Palestine to-day. The frontier is not here, but some hours' journey farther east, at El Arish, where the torrent that we read of in the Bible as the " River of Egypt " descends from Sinai.

The railway and the Canal run side by side as far as Ismailia, on Lake Timsah. Here, again, is a town which owes its being to the Canal, which, like Port Said, depends for its water supply on the fresh-water canal that de Lesseps made. But Ismailia has so much more beauty about it and has been so well laid out that it is much harder to realize that it has all been reclaimed from the desert.

The charming, but somewhat exclusive, colony of French officials that inhabit it does not much encourage visitors, but I was once fortunate enough to be the guest of some French friends who lived in a delightful bungalow, where, from the back veranda, we could watch the barges on the fresh-water

canal ; and, from the front we could see over tall, dark trees
to the blue lake and the desert hills on the farther side. Every
afternoon the colony gathered at the bathing beach, where, in
the warm and briny water, the weakest swimmer can venture
without fear. Then, at sundown, a motor-launch took us
out upon the lake and gay talk and song went on till the stars
shone out in the clear sky and the merry party landed again,
to be driven home in a big yellow motor, affectionately termed
le péril jaune. A delightful place is this little bit of France
dropped down in the desert, but far removed from any other
aspect of Egypt that I have come across.

From Ismailia the railway turns inland, over the desert,
and soon, if we chance to look out at a wayside station, we
may see a graveyard, with the names of English soldiers on
the headstones. This is Tell el Kebir, where Wolseley defeated
Arabi Pasha and put an end to the rebellion of 1882. Arabi's
revolt was very, very pardonable. The abuses of government
by the Turkish rulers of Egypt were gross and notorious, and
most of the Europeans who were helping Ismail to squeeze
the country dry were of the most unscrupulous class. Had
Arabi been a stronger man and a real national leader, the
course of history might have run differently, but he was
vacillating, weak and devoid of any governing faculty. The
movement had carried him away and had become, instead of
a revolt against Turkish misrule, an insurrection of a violently
anti-Christian, as well as anti-foreign character. The Coptic
population—always a considerable minority—were in great
danger and the large Levantine community, who were mostly
protected by the Capitulations with the European Powers,
felt that their Governments and Consuls were helpless, and
were flying from Egypt as fast as they could get boats to
carry them.

Many European Powers were pledged to support the dynasty
of Mehemet Aly ; all of them, under the Capitulations, had
received pledges from Turkey for the safety of their subjects
trading and settling in her dominions : why then should
England alone have had to step in and take military action ?
Why, when she did step in and take practical possession of

Egypt, did she stop short of taking avowed possession ? It
is a complicated and interesting question, depending partly on
the personalities in power at the time in England, partly upon
general European politics. For a full and fair discussion of
it, readers are referred to Lord Milner's " England in Egypt,"
and to Chapters XVI and XVII of Lord Cromer's " Modern
Egypt."

After Tell el Kebir, there was no doubt that England had to
take vigorous action to avoid the anarchy that was impending
over the helpless and bankrupt country. No risk must be
taken of a repetition on a larger scale of what had happened in
Alexandria for want of a regular occupation of the town after
the bombardment ; also the chance of the water supply being
cut off must be guarded against promptly, for all this tract of
desert depends for its water on the fresh-water canal, which is
taken off from the Nile near Bilbeis.

A small force of cavalry was at once pushed on to Cairo. On
September 14, 1882, the Citadel was occupied and a better day
began to dawn for the sorely afflicted Egyptian fellah.

The railway runs, for the first part of the way, up the Wady
Tumilat, once the land of Goshen, which was given to the
Children of Israel for their place of sojourn in the country.
A much older canal was here at that time, for the problem
of joining the Nile to the Red Sea was very present to the
ancient Egyptians. Probably the canal was first cut in the
Middle Empire, about 2,000 B.C., but as it often was neglected
and silted up, it was repeatedly cleared again by later rulers,
who all took credit for the original digging out.

All the way up to Cairo the cultivation we pass through
tells the tale of what a steady government and a good water
supply have done for the material prosperity of the country.
Round Zagazig is a great cotton-growing area, and, though
even in the fat, fertile Delta there are differences of level which
affect the yield of crop, the land now supports a population
nearly three times as large as it did fifty years ago. The
irrigation of the Delta depends on the Barrage, a dam built
across the two arms of the Nile where it divides a few miles
below Cairo. It was made by French engineers under Mehemet

3

Aly, but had never been taken full advantage of and had fallen entirely out of working order. One of the first problems for the English engineers who took office in Egypt was whether the Barrage could be repaired, and if so, how they could face the expense of doing it.   Lord Milner, in his " England in Egypt," gives a vivid account of these early years of anxiety, when they not only had to administer the impoverished country, but to squeeze out interest for the bondholders.   His description of the hand-to-mouth economies resorted to, and the mixture of tragedy and comedy of the whole situation is fascinating reading.   In fact, the book is indispensable to anyone who wants to realize the complications at the beginning of the English occupation.   He always makes us see what is always there in Egypt, the comic-opera side of solemn events. I feel sure that pulled the hard-worked officials through many of the early troubles !   It was a dreadful situation : the people, industrious, sober, docile, but starving, with the means of plenty all round, requiring only a little honesty and a little outlay to bring back an abundant return, but not a penny in the Treasury to lay out on it.   Everything was out of order and needed money to set it right, but nearly everything had to wait.   However, there was one thing on which they dared not save.   The whole of Egypt's future depended on the irrigation, and, to get the water system put in order, money must be got somehow.   So the repair of the Barrage was carried out and has proved a great success.

At present, I understand, good cotton land lets at £20 or £25 an acre per annum.   As there are very many estates of four and five hundred acres, and some much larger, it is evident that great fortunes have become common.   The landholders are almost all Egyptians ; a few belong to the old class of Turkish Pashas, but far more are enriched fellahin whose fathers worked on the land.   This wealth has poured in so quickly that it is only natural that the younger generation has not begun to feel any of the responsibilities which, in another state of society, are generally attached to the administration of property, especially property in land.   A house in Cairo or Alexandria, motor-cars, European watering-places, gambling at cards, horses and the Bourse, fill the lives of the young and rich Egyptians, while those of more moderate means go to Europe to study and enjoy themselves and come back to Egypt to go into politics. I do not think it occurs to any of them to take an interest in their tenants or labourers, and the thought of living in the country is repugnant to every cultivated mind. But among the old-fashioned landlords there is a more patriarchal state of things. The men of the village assemble nightly on the veranda of the rich man's house to discuss village and national politics, the rotation of crops and the prices of commodities. It is a democratic sort of life, with the democracy of Islam, which by no means excludes oppression and cruelty, but inculcates courtesy, and, because the women are secluded, does make for a certain equality of the men.

It is, of course, the landholders who have benefited so enormously by the English occupation, but the lot of the fellah of to-day, who labours on the land without owning any of it, is greatly better than it used to be. The cotton crop provides work for the whole family. The children are employed during most of the summer in picking off the insect pests which attack the plants, and they and the women do the most of the gathering in autumn. The cotton is sown about March and gathered in September and October, so that few tourists ever see it on the ground. It is an exhausting crop and it is only legally permissible to grow it every third year, but there are ways by which this may be evaded, and year by year there is probably a good deal more than a third of the land under cotton. The rotations are various, but a favourite one is : cotton, beans, bersim (a kind of clover which makes a rich fodder), millet or maize, wheat, another crop of bersim, this time often ploughed in as a fertilizer, and cotton again. In the north of the Delta a great deal of rice is grown.

In spite of the increase in prosperity, the outward aspect of the villages has not altered much and is terribly squalid. The towns, on the other hand, although they are very uninviting to look at, have visible evidences of wealth and progress compared with twenty years ago. Tanta, Mansoura and

Zagazig have more than doubled in size and possess municipalities, hospitals, schools for boys and girls and much better houses than they used to have. But they are depressingly ugly. Perhaps the total lack of any beauty or picturesqueness is due to the large Greek element in the population. The modern Greek will plant his sordid little towns in the most beautiful situations, with absolutely no regard for the surroundings ; and, if he can set up his hideous streets and houses in sight of Ida and Olympus, what can one expect from him on the dull Egyptian plain ?

The Greek is ubiquitous. He keeps the station refreshment rooms, the village café and the grocer's shop ; lives as frugally as his neighbours but is quicker witted and better educated ; he is protected by his Consul, pays no taxes, is, in short, in an excellent position for making money. He lends a little here and a little there, on the security of the next crops ; gradually grows rich and moves on to wider spheres, but another takes his place and works in with him, so that it comes about that a large part of the commerce of Egypt is in Greek hands. He does not grow the cotton, but he buys and sells it and deals in every other commodity, legal or illegal, that comes and goes to and from Egypt.

The ancient sites of the Delta must not be omitted from any description, but they are much less in evidence than formerly. They are marked by low mounds of brick, sometimes apart from any dwellings of the present day, but nearly always to be found in the vicinity, or underneath the modern towns, for these unattractive collections of houses generally have a long history behind them. The reason why the mounds are lower than they used to be is rather curious. The brick remains, mixed with the organic refuse they contain, seems to have a definite value as manure and is much prized by the fellahin, who are allowed to remove it, under certain restrictions, to put on their fields. I am assured that its value is much overrated, but the concessions to carry it away are eagerly sought for and a large part of the work of the Antiquities officials is the endeavour to protect their ancient sites. Also, if a man's fields just border one of these mounds, what

more tempting and more easy than to enlarge his holding by
cultivating a few yards of the old mound, which never could
be missed ? This is a temptation that no fellah ever thinks of
resisting, so it is evident that the end of the mound would not
be long deferred if inspection were not constant and efficient.

Some twenty-odd years ago, I paid a visit to Zagazig which
left two strong impressions on my mind. I dare say the place
is better now, but I do not believe there is much improvement
on the shabby Greek inn where we stayed, in a room divided
from the next one only by a thin partition which did not
reach the roof, with washing arrangements of the sketchiest,
and oily, Greek food at a neighbouring restaurant. But when
we left the bustling, dirty Zagazig of the present and walked
over the dusty mounds that border it, we were suddenly in
Bubastis of the past and out of sight and hearing of the
modern town.

The Bubastis mound was once very high, and in its centre was
a deep hollow, where stood the great temple of the goddess
Bast, one of the chiefest of Egyptian deities. It was built
of massive blocks of stone, while the town round about it was
of crude brick, as Egyptian towns always are and always were.
Thus it came about that the temple stood firm on the solid
ground, but the surrounding houses fell into ruin and others
were built above them. When Herodotus saw it in the
fifth century B.C. he describes this feature :

" Bubastis, in the Grecian language, answers to Diana.
Her sacred precinct is thus situated : all except the entrance
is an island ; for two canals from the Nile extend to it . . .
one flowing round it on one side, the other on the other.
Each is a hundred feet broad and shaded with trees. The
portico is ten orgyæ in height, and is adorned with figures
six cubits high, that are deserving of notice. This precinct,
being in the middle of the city, is visible on every side to a
person going round it : for as the city has been mounded up
to a considerable height, but the temple has not been moved,
it is conspicuous as it was originally built."

His account of the festival of Bubastis is extremely interesting, as there seems no doubt that this fantasía and most of the customs connected with it have been transferred to Tanta, and are now celebrated in honour of Sidi Ahmed el Bedawi, the most popular of Muslim saints. His birthday is in August, when a great Fair is held, attracting hosts of pilgrims, in numbers perhaps equal to Herodotus' seven hundred thousand, and in practices not very different, except that they go by train and not by boat. Herodotus says :

" Now, when they are being conveyed to the city Bubastis, they act in the following manner : for men and women embark together, and great numbers of both sexes in every barge : some of the women have castanets on which they play, and the men play on the flute during the whole voyage ; the rest of the women and men sing and clap their hands together at the same time. When in the course of their passage they come to any town, they lay their barge near to land, and do as follows : some of the women do as I have described ; others shout and scoff at the women of the place, some dance, and others stand up and pull up their clothes : this they do at every town by the river side. When they arrive at Bubastis, they celebrate the feast, offering up great sacrifices ; and more wine is consumed at this festival than in all the rest of the year. What with men and women, beside children, they congregate, as the inhabitants say, to the number of seven hundred thousand."

The Tanta mosque in itself, is a poor goal for the procession, compared with what the splendid temple of Bubastis must have been, though not one stone of it is left standing on another. Great scattered and fallen columns strew the ground, granite blocks with the names of famous Pharaohs lie half hidden among rushes and salty pools, the wild birds flap around and shrilly shriek. I have never seen any place that gave a more dreary feeling of utter desolateness.

" The cormorant and the bittern shall possess it, the owl also and the raven shall dwell in it . . . thorns shall come up in her palaces, nettles and brambles in the fortresses thereof . . . there shall the great owl make her nest and lay and hatch and gather under her shadow; there shall the vulture also be gathered, every one with her mate."

All around is the desolation of plundered and deserted human habitations, long, long dead and forsaken ; a dreariness I have never seen equalled. But it had a glory once.

CHAPTER III

THE PYRAMIDS

"LES Pyramides ? Ça, c'est au bout du tramway," said a French lady to a friend of mine, unconsciously voicing the point of view of a great many Cairene residents, who look upon the Pyramid plateau as a good place for an excursion, perfectly oblivious of the fact that there may be something to be looked for there of a different order of interest.

I suppose it must have been much more impressive to see the Pyramids thirty or forty years ago, when there was no tram and one went by carriage from Cairo, or better still, when there was no road and no Nile bridge, and one crossed in a ferry boat to Giza and rode out the six miles from there on donkeys or camels. But it is a standing marvel to me how little all the changes have been able to vulgarize the place. The electric tramway stops beside the big hotel at the foot of the slope, motors hoot up it and deposit their burdens at the very base of the Great Pyramid ; a regular Bank-holiday crowd of Levantines pours out from Cairo every Sunday, and yet, hardly do we pass round the corner of the pyramid than the silence of the desert gets hold of us. It is very good to get away from the guides and the dragomans and think about it quietly. Perhaps the best thing of all is to stay out at Mena House or to camp near by and so be able to go about and see the morning lights, the sunset and the moon, and grow familiar with the mighty cemetery in all its aspects, but one can make excellent expeditions from Cairo by taxi or tram, and there is nothing more rewarding.

The drive out is interesting, passing the Zoological Gardens,

PLATE I

PYRAMID PLATEAU FROM THE AIR

which are delightful. There is a sheet of water inside, stocked with pelicans and rare breeds of waterfowl, where the night herons roost in the trees and annual crowds of wild duck find a safe retreat every winter season. Beyond this is Giza village, and, when it is left behind, the road runs westwards through the cultivation. Before the Assuan dam was made, all this country used to be flooded in the autumn, and a very beautiful sight it was, with the villages rising out of the waters, as Herodotus says, " like the islands in the Ægean." There is still a line of flooded basins near the desert edge, and the traveller is lucky who comes early enough to see the Pyramids reflected in the water below. The first half of November is generally safe, and is a beautiful time of year to be in Cairo, but there is no fixed date for the emptying of the basins ; it is settled each year by the Irrigation Department as circumstances require.

To many people, the first sight of the Pyramids is the first sight of the desert also, and the place seems overpowering. The desert will grow familiar, but I think the Pyramids get more and more tremendous the more we see of them. The wonder never passes, but interest deepens greatly if one comes to understand something about them. There are two main points to be kept in mind : commonplaces, no doubt, to those acquainted with Egypt and the antiquities, but seldom realized by new-comers. Firstly, that an Egyptian grave has two parts ; one for the dead and one for the living ; secondly, that the Pyramids are always royal graves ; graves of kings and queens, and, that all the tombs which surround them are the graves of noblemen and their dependents.

Nowhere can these statements be better verified than at Giza (see Pl. I). The interior of the pyramid is the actual burying-place where the royal mummy was laid to rest. The entrance was carefully concealed and the dead king was left, never to be disturbed, it was hoped, to all eternity. But his spirit was not to be confined there. The non-material part of him could leave the tomb and roam, like his father the Sun, across the sky and join the company of the gods. Yet, he still depended, for his continued existence, upon the offerings

of his faithful subjects on earth, so the other part of the tomb
had to be provided. Every pyramid had a temple on the east
side, where services were carried on by specially dedicated
priests and where public processions of worshippers assembled
and took part in the ritual. A causeway led from the edge
of the desert up to the temple, and, at the lower end of it was
another temple, a sort of palatial gateway, which, in flood
time made a landing-place for boats.

The tombs of private people are quite different. There, the
burial was at the bottom of a deep shaft. The body was
placed there, enclosed in a massive stone sarcophagus and
the shaft was filled up. But, again, the spirit was not impris-
oned in the vault. The life principle that was in the man
did not perish, but, so long as his memory remained on earth
and offerings were brought to sustain him, his personality
went on. A house was built above the burial shaft ; here at
Giza, generally an erection of solid stone, but always with the
semblance of a door inserted in the masonry, and often with
a little decorated chapel for the funerary services. The door
was for the spirit to pass through, when he came to feed on
the offerings and to benefit by the magic ritual performed by
the priests of the tomb and by his living descendants.

Cheops, the builder of the Great Pyramid, designed the
whole cemetery east and west of his own great tomb, so that
his family and his courtiers should have their places near him.
Recent discoveries by Dr. Reisner of Harvard, who has lived
for many years on the Giza plateau and made a very thorough
study of the problems of the Pyramids, have thrown much
light on the arrangement of these graves. Just to the east
of Cheops' pyramid are the three little pyramids of his queens,
below them, towards the cultivation, are rows of " mastaba "
tombs belonging to members of his family. To the west of
the pyramid the nobles and people of his Court are buried.

The Second and Third Pyramids, where Cheops' successors,
Chephren and Mycerinus, are buried, also have tombs of
their nobles near them, but they are much less regularly disposed than those round the Great Pyramid. A leading fact
about all the Pyramid plateau is, that practically everything

belongs to the same period ; the great Fourth Dynasty, at the beginning of what is known as the Old Empire.

Dr. Reisner has been working in the season of 1924-5 on the area we reach almost as soon as we come to the top of the plateau. First of all, however, is a modern house, which was built by Ismail Pasha to receive the Empress of the French on the day of her visit to the Pyramids, when she was in Egypt for the opening of the Suez Canal. Then, a few yards to the left, overlooking the beautiful view of Cairo and the green valley, and we are in the cemetery of Cheops' family. The temple of the Great Pyramid has been utterly destroyed ; only a few black blocks in the roadway remind us that its pavement was of basalt, but Dr. Reisner has uncovered part of the foundations of the Causeway, about which Herodotus says that it was " a work, in my opinion, not much less than the pyramid."

Close to the causeway is a deep trench, shaped like a boat, in which, when the king was buried, a great wooden ship, the Barque of the Sun, was interred likewise, so that, when the spirit of the dead king should leave his pyramid, he might voyage across the heavens with his father.

This important discovery is quite a new feature at Giza, and may shed fresh light on the ritual of the pyramid age. A smaller but similar trench has been found near the pyramid of one of the queens. Plate I, a photograph taken from the air, gives an excellent general view of the plateau and is worth looking at carefully.

Mena House Hotel, with its gardens, is at the foot of the picture, and the road up to the Great Pyramid is seen winding above it. Behind the Great Pyramid are the lines of mastaba tombs, built by Cheops for his noblemen and courtiers. Beyond, the Second and Third Pyramids, with their temples on the eastern side are clearly shown. The tombs of Cheops' queens and of his children and descendants are to the east of the pyramid and just out of the picture.

Underneath this part of the cemetery, and thus protected from robbery, is the tomb of the Third Dynasty, which has been one of the sensational discoveries of the past season

(1924–5). It has been a great surprise to find that there was
anything on the Giza plateau earlier than the Pyramids and the
fact that it is, to all appearance, an undisturbed tomb, renders
it a matter of the highest importance. Dr. Reisner, who had
gone to attend to duties in America, leaving the excavation
to be carried on by his assistants, has not yet (June, 1925),
returned to Egypt, but his presence is necessary for the clearing
and recording of the tomb. So at present, all that can be
stated with certainty is that the tomb contains a fine sarcophagus of alabaster, and on it an object bearing the name of
Seneferu, the last king of the Third Dynasty and, probably,
the immediate predecessor of Cheops. There is also funerary
furniture which will be of great interest, although it is feared
that it is not in good condition. It is not probable that this
is the tomb of Seneferu himself. Much more likely that the
sarcophagus was a gift from him to a relative or to a favourite
official, for Seneferu has already two pyramids ascribed to
him, and can hardly be credited with yet another burying-
place ! But there is no doubt about the great importance of
the find, and the results of Dr. Reisner's investigations are
awaited with eagerness.

Passing the Great Pyramid and this cemetery, we come to
the Sphinx and the group of buildings belonging to the Second
Pyramid.

I have never been able to understand why people were so
thrilled about the Sphinx and the mystery of it. Perhaps it
has become mixed up with the sphinx of Œdipus and its
riddle ; and, as all the writers on Egypt used to say that
no one knew who the Sphinx represented, the idea of mystery
has grown round its image.

But the mystery of the origin of the Great Sphinx has been
dispelled of recent years, for it proves to be the work of the
very king who would most naturally be connected with it,
Chephren or Khafra, the builder of the Second Pyramid, and,
by his works, one of the greatest artists of Egypt. Whether
all these were due to him, or whether he had in his employ a
man of genius, who showed him what he could do to make
manifest his divinity before the face of his subjects, no one

can ever tell, but the works remain ; the pyramid, its temple
lined with granite from Assuan and basalt from the Delta
quarries, and the Valley or Gateway temple, at the foot of
the causeway, built all of massive granite blocks. A mighty
temple this, but somewhat overshadowed, it may have been,
by a huge rock which rose above it and suggested that Nature's
building might even surpass the Pharaoh's. This seeming
difficulty and drawback was converted into a great opportunity, for Chephren subdued it to his will and to his greater
glory by carving the whole rocky headland into a likeness
of himself, figured as the Sun god, embodying in his image
the strength of the lion and the wisdom of man. It is sorely
battered now and weathered by the winds and the drifting
sand. Nature has got the worst of it for once, and Chephren's
pyramid towers above, clear cut against the sky, while the
gigantic features of the Sphinx are worn away and the en-
croaching sand has covered its colossal paws. Round the
Sphinx one is beset by photographers and dealers in faked
antiquities, yet, if one can only find the place in quietness,
it is an imposing sight, and no one should be content with
merely looking down into the Valley temple from above,
for the interior is, to my thinking, one of the grandest things
in Egypt. Imagine this temple with its roof of stone and
floor of alabaster : replace in it in thought the diorite statue
of Chephren from the Museum and the two and twenty other
statues of the king that formed its sole adornment, and, what
a picture it conjures up of august solemnity ! From it we
pass up the line of the old causeway, once a corridor, roofed
and lined with Tura limestone, to the temple right up against
the eastern wall of the pyramid, and there, for a peaceful hour
or two, we may rest ; or, if we like to go still farther afield
in search of peace, we may go on to the temple of the Third
Pyramid, where there are massive ruins, and, perhaps, an even
finer view.

Here, sitting in the shade, we have a tranquil time to read
our guide-books, or just to look and enjoy and try to realize
the place. I don't think that one wants to be told much
about the date and the dimensions of the Pyramids for a

while. We have got to take them in mentally, their immensity, their strangeness and the strangeness of the narrow land. The Pyramids have something of the quality and calm of the everlasting things ; the desert, or the hills, or the " multi- tudinous stars that said We are steadfast, we are not as ye." They have stood changeless these thousands of years, while the generations of men, toiling, fighting, rejoicing, despairing, have breathed and passed away. All the world's history has rolled by since they were built, and we strain across the gulf to feel for a human touch to tell us if these men, who lighted the scarce kindled torch of human progress to a brighter flame, were indeed men of like passions with ourselves. It is too far off to tell. Without the written word it is hard to find any trace of the soul that guided the deeds of men, and, these old citizens of Memphis and Helio- polis, who, by their labour, devised the art of writing and gave it to the world, themselves wrote very little that is of help to us. We can only stand amazed before their works. Some little, indeed, we can learn from these, of the manner of men they were and the lives they led, for, because of their careful- ness for the future, their art was made to endure ; the pyra- mids to be the royal sepulchres, sculptures to keep their faces in remembrance ; above all, the storied walls of their tombs which glow with every scene of varied life. From what is seen there it is possible to get back to the outward aspect of things, at least in some measure, and it is worth while trying to picture what sort of life and landscape we should have looked out on had we been sitting at this temple door five thousand years ago, when the pyramids were new.

The country cannot have altered much in general contour, for the desert is unchanging and dead, and there was always the same narrow strip of fertile land between the Libyan and the Arabian hills. But there are differences. For one thing, the desert then was not quite so dead. It is rather difficult to say how it has happened, but there was much more vegetation long ago, enough to support a large amount of game, where now there is hardly anything alive but jackals and foxes, a few hyenas, and, farther out, some gazelle and a very few ibex. In the pyramid age there were gazelle and ibex in abundance, several kinds of antelopes, a rare stag or two, and even lions, for nobody can draw a lion, certainly not a recognizable lion, without having seen one ; and there are very good lions in some of the tombs at Sakkara. It was evidently rather a prize to get one. When captured, the lion was brought along in a cage and probably kept afterwards as a trophy, but all the other animals, even hyenas, were used for food and were kept in pens and fattened up until required.

The fertile land, similarly, was less fertile, and there was far more wild life about than at the present day. An irrigation system had been introduced by the time the Pyramids were built ; the flood was already regulated by sluices and basins, no doubt in a primitive sort of way, but in principle, by the same methods as were used down to very recent times. But the system did not extend over all the present area of Egypt ; the cultivated ground was only to be found near the river, while on the desert edge, the water rose and fell again unregulated. The consequence was that pools of water and marshes remained all the year round near the desert, replenished every autumn by the inundation, but never quite drying up. These marshy places were thickly overgrown with papyrus and teemed with crocodile, hippopotamus and every kind of wild bird. Lanes of open water were made through the dense papyrus groves for the boats to go and come, little boats of twisted papyrus—arks of bulrushes—in which the nobleman and his servants went hunting and fishing. The Old Empire people were great sportsmen and there was plenty of very exciting sport. I am not sure whether the great man ever risked his life going after the hippopotamus, or whether he watched it from a safe distance. A most dangerous sport it must have been, hunting hippos from a reed boat. The hunters threw a harpoon and slipped away, giving out rope as they went ; each harpoon had a sort of tassel hanging to it which floated on the water and showed where the hippo was, so that they could fix another and another into him till he got wearied out.

When going after birds for pleasure, the great man used a

boomerang and, for fish, a spear ; to believe the pictures his success was phenomenal, but countless numbers of birds were caught and trapped for food in less sportsmanlike fashion, by means of a large net which was spread in the marsh. The birds were brought home and kept in cages ; fish were caught in small or large nets according to the depth of the pools. Most of them were salted and preserved in jars.

Not only were the hunters exposed to considerable danger in the course of their pursuits, but the unlucky herdsmen who had to drive the cattle across these shallow bits of water to their grazing ground, went in terror of their lives from the crocodiles. When this scene is depicted in the tombs, there is generally written above it the words of the charm against the crocodile which they chanted as they went over.

The house of the great lord for whose benefit all this was done was some distance away. Owing to the inundation which laid the country under water for three months of every year, the inhabitants must always have lived in towns or villages, raised above the level of the surrounding fields. On the desert, of course, it was safe from wet, and there are a good many remains of early settlements there, but I do not think that very many people lived on the desert, beyond the considerable population that was employed in building and guarding the tombs. The desert was then, as it is to-day, the natural burying-place, the dwelling of the dead, but not of the living.

The town was Memphis, which stretched for miles along the Nile, to the south of Giza, but whereabout the palaces of the pyramid kings may have been, it is not possible to say. The houses and the palaces were of mud brick, for a man never squandered fine stone on his abode for the brief span of his life on earth ; the stone house built for lasting was up on the desert and was furnished with all he would need for eternity.

They made their houses for this transient world, however, as comfortable as they could : from the pictures and from the few objects that have survived the forty-five odd centuries that separate us from them, we know that among the furniture there were beds, tables, chairs, rugs, chests, beautifully woven linen, jewellery, jars of pottery and vases of stone, and that their abundant meals consisted of meat and game, geese and quail, bread, onions, figs and pomegranates, washed down with beer, wine and milk.

The methods of cultivation were not much more primitive than what we may see in use to-day and the domestic animals were the same, if we except the horse and the camel. The horse did not come to Egypt till the Hyksos period, more than a thousand years after the pyramids, and the camel, probably, not until much later, but this is a disputed point. There were several breeds of cows, sheep and goats and any number of donkeys, though these were only used, it would appear, as beasts of burden; I do not remember a picture of a donkey being ridden by man, woman or child in the Old Empire. People walked where they wanted to go, except the lord himself, who was carried about in his arm-chair slung on poles, to see his fields, or up to the desert to inspect the progress of his tomb.

What a scene it must have been when the king himself came up in state to see his pyramid and to watch the armies of workmen he kept hauling the stone for it and hoisting the blocks into place!

We get some guide to this in Herodotus, who saw the pyramids standing, externally still in all their glory, though they had been robbed and the royal mummies destroyed long before. He picked up all the tales he could as to the way they were built and the legends that were current about them. But it was two thousand years after the pyramid age that he was there; he was a foreigner and had to get all his information through an interpreter, so it is no wonder that his stories are not to be depended on as history, but they are of unique interest, for they tell us something of what the Egyptians in his time thought about their far-away past. And Herodotus was an excellent observer; the things he reports as having seen with his own eyes are on an entirely different level of trustworthiness. It is all delightful reading. Herodotus, the first traveller in Egypt, has written what is

easily the best book about it, and I cannot refrain from
quoting some of his descriptions.

"Cheops became king over them and brought them to
every kind of evil : for he shut up all the temples, and having
first kept them from sacrifices there, he then bade all the
Egyptians work for him. So some were appointed to draw
stones from the stone quarries in the Arabian mountains to
the Nile, and others he ordered to receive the stones after they
had been carried over the river in boats, and to draw them to
those which are called the Libyan mountains ; and they
worked by a hundred thousand men at a time, for each three
months continually. Of this oppression there passed ten
years while the causeway was made by which they drew the
stones, which causeway they built, and it is a work not much
less, as it appears to me, than the pyramid ; for the length of
it is five furlongs and the breadth ten fathoms and the height,
where it is highest, eight fathoms, and it is made of stone
smoothed and with figures carved upon it."

Then he has an inexplicable bit about a channel from the
Nile, which must have been a dragoman's tale ; I don't
understand how Herodotus could have swallowed it, as it
seems obviously impossible. He goes on, "For the making
of the pyramid itself there passed a period of twenty years,"
which is a moderate and very probable estimate. Sir Flinders
Petrie thinks that the hundred thousand men were only
employed to bring the stone from Tura during the inundation,
when they would not be working in the fields, and has worked
out with much ingenuity the number of men that would be
required to quarry and transport each of the two and a half
million blocks that are calculated to be in the Great Pyramid.
Herodotus next goes on to say what he learned about the
building :

"This pyramid was made after the manner of steps, which
some call ' rows ' and others ' bases,' and when they had first
made it thus, they raised the remaining stones with machines
made of short pieces of timber, raising them first from the
ground to the first stage of the steps, and when the stone got

up to this it was placed upon another machine standing on the first stage, and so from this it was drawn to the second upon another machine ; for as many as were the courses of the steps, so many machines there were also, or perhaps they transferred one and the same machine, made so as easily to be carried, to each stage successively, in order that they might take up the stones ; for let it be told in both ways according as it is reported. However that may be, the highest parts of it were finished first, and afterwards they proceeded to finish that which came next to them, and lastly they finished the parts of it near the ground and the lowest ranges. On the pyramid it is declared in Egyptian writing how much was spent on radishes and onions and leeks for the workmen, and if I rightly remember that which the interpreter said to me in reading this inscription, a sum of one thousand six hundred talents of silver was spent."

No one can make very much of the " machine made of short pieces of timber," and the problem of how the pyramids were built is by no means yet solved, but Dr. Reisner has tried many experiments with his trained gangs of Egyptian workmen to see what could be done with man power and the very simplest of tackle. His results have not yet been given to the public, but there can be no doubt that the solution lies in that direction : man power, unlimited man power, and little else. About the Second Pyramid, Herodotus says :

" This king followed the same manner of dealing as the other, both in all the rest and also in that he made a pyramid, not indeed attaining to the measurements of that which was built by the former " (this I know, having myself measured it) . . . " but for a basement he built the first course of Ethiopian stone of divers colours ; and this pyramid he made forty feet lower than the other as regards size, building it close to the Great Pyramid. These stand both upon the same hill, which is about a hundred feet high. And Chephren they said, reigned fifty and six years."

After this Herodotus goes off into entertaining but unquotable tales about Mycerinus, the builder of the Third Pyramid, and other Pharaohs, and gets down in time to the history of the Persian kings who were in power when he came to Egypt. There has never been any Egyptian history so readable: perhaps the critical faculty has developed too far in our day and we trouble too much about contemporary documents and archæological evidence and never take Herodotus' plan, which is so convenient and so suggestive, and say " This story I know, but it is not a seemly one for me to tell," or, " If I should say for what reason " such and such a thing was done " I should fall into discourse of matters pertaining to the gods."

But some plain matter-of-fact statements we can make with more certainty than Herodotus could, for the language is no longer a mystery and archæological research has thrown a flood of light upon the early world. He saw what tremendous works the pyramids were, but he could not know that they were not only the biggest buildings in the world, but that they were also the first. It is staggering to think that a couple of centuries before the Great Pyramid, men did not build in stone at all. Sitting here on the Giza plateau we can see the oldest of them ; the Step Pyramid of Sakkara and the tips of the two large pyramids of Dahshur, all of which were there before the Great Pyramid, but only a generation or two before.

The reason of this amazing new departure was that metal had just begun to be worked in large quantities. It was the copper mines of Sinai that made the quarries of Tura possible. But it was not only Tura that was laid under contribution ; granite was brought from distant Assuan for the adornment of the temples and the casing of the Third Pyramid.

There had been centuries of slow progress before this, it is true, but as soon as they gained the free use of metals, the expansion was marvellously quick. And there must have been great, very great leadership. These kings of the Fourth Dynasty were gods to themselves and to their people and they reared godlike dwellings for their spirits, where posterity for ages to come should gather to worship and the chant of hymns and the odour of offerings should never cease.

The songs fell silent, the ritual failed, the royal mummies

close shut within the solid stone were plundered long, long ago, but the mighty masonry stands, unshattered by Time and raging anarchy without.

The Old Empire fell, the capital was changed, the pyramid worship was abandoned, but a thousand years later, when the Children of Israel were in bondage in the land, the pyramids were still unimpaired. Another millennium, and the Egyptians had turned again to the worship of their ancient kings and did many works of repair and restoration on the temples and tombs. Again a blank of more than two thousand years falls over them, when they were once more forgotten and neglected, but the worst of the damage that has befallen them does not seem to have happened until the Middle Ages, when the town of Cairo was growing up. The Muslim builders stripped off the outer casings, all except the little tip that remains on Chephren's pyramid ; and the tombs of Cheops' nobles were wrecked wherever the sand had not blown over and protected them.

We can see bits of sculpture from these tombs built into the walls of Cairo, and, it is said that the great mosque of Sultan Hassan was built from the casing blocks of the Great Pyramid.

But after all, the quarrying and the plundering of the pyramids is something like the desolation wrought by a fire on a mountain-side, a scar and a disfigurement, but not a destruction. They are the only survivors of the seven wonders of the ancient world and they surely will survive still, stark and immense, when other Empires and other civilizations have passed away.

They

> " Tell the conqueror,
> That far-stretched power,
> Which his proud dangers traffic for,
> Is but the triumph of an hour."

CHAPTER IV

THE EGYPTIAN MUSEUM

ABOUT the year 1850, under the Khedive Abbas, Mariette a French scholar, came to Egypt with the view of studying Coptic Manuscripts in some of the monasteries of the country. Delays and difficulties occurred in his getting the necessary facilities to be allowed to see all he wanted, and he decided instead, to go to Sakkara and make observations. Things of interest were to be seen there, though, compared with what there now is, there must have been extremely little. No systematic search had ever been made, but it was known to be the cemetery of Memphis. It had been robbed without intermission from the most ancient times and quantities of antiquities were always, truly or falsely, said to have come from there. Mariette was convinced of the great possibilities of the site and determined to give all the time and care that he could to investigating it. He noticed one or two little sphinxes of Greek workmanship sticking up through the sand, which recalled to him a passage in Strabo to the effect that the road leading to the Serapeum of Sakkara was bordered by sphinxes. He set to work to trace this out, and so began one of the romances of archæology. It all came true beyond his wildest dreams, for he lighted on the very avenue of sphinxes that led to the great Serapeum, he passed through the cavernous gateway to the vaults and explored their vast, dark recesses, came on one huge sarcophagus after another, each wrought from a single block of massive basalt. Parts of the walls were covered with inscribed stelæ ; the very floors were littered with bones and linen and gold leaf which had been dropped by the plunderers

42

of former days. It was colossal, gloomy and awesome beyond
words. And, evidently, it was far too big a thing for Mariette
to tackle with the small funds at his disposal ; besides, it was
clearly a matter of national importance to Egypt, so Mariette
betook himself to the Khedive and represented to him the
glory and profit that would accrue to Egypt from the excavation of such a monument. The Khedive was sympathetic
and helpful. A regular budget was not thought of at first,
but he gave Mariette at times a grant of money, at other times
a *corvée* of workmen, perhaps 500 or 1,000 men at a time for a
month or two. Mariette was thus enabled to turn over an
enormous amount of ground, to uncover a number of Old
Empire tombs of the highest importance and, incidentally,
to find some absolutely priceless statues.

The stelæ found in the Serapeum at the beginning of the
digging had been presented to the Louvre by the Khedive,
but during the subsequent years Egypt was supplying all
the funds for excavation and obviously must keep a good
proportion of the objects found, so it became necessary to
provide some building in which they could be well preserved
and suitably shown. In this way the Service des Antiquités
came into being, for a Museum implied a curator and staff
and a budget for their salaries, apart from the expenses of
the outside work.

Many antiquities had left Egypt before that time, for it
had been a policy of Mehemet Aly's to placate the foreign
consuls with *douceurs* in the shape of permission to dig and
export antiquities. The collections acquired in this manner
by Salt, Drovetti and other European consuls form the nucleus
of most of those in the great national Museums of Europe.
Other people, like Belzoni, excavated with much enthusiasm
at the cost of the consuls, with the sporting chance of being
able to get a good thing on their own account as well. And,
of course, tourists bought objects which interested them
and which they believed they were getting cheaply. There
must have been a considerable demand for small antiquities
by the people on dahabiehs even by the middle of the nineteenth century, for it is surprising to see how many forgeries

there usually are in these old collections, bought, one would
have imagined, before it had occurred to the inhabitants of
Luxor to try their hands at imitations.

But these early finds fade into insignificance before the
discoveries of Mariette. He worked in the Egyptian service
more or less continuously for more than twenty years, and
from Sakkara and other sites, brought to light a material so
rich that it changed all previous conceptions of Egyptian art.

The first Museum where the objects were lodged was at
Boulac, in a small building near the Nile, which is said to
have been well lighted and well arranged, but it soon became
too small for the increasing volume of antiquities that poured
in. Foreign excavators had begun to undertake work also,
and a certain proportion of all the finds belonged to the
Egyptian Government. The collection was removed to a
Palace of Ismail Pasha's at Giza, which was large enough, but
was an ill-constructed barrack, anything but fireproof, and
it was most incongruous to see the massive Egyptian sculptures
among the gilding and mirrors of the Palace. But round
about was a beautiful park and it is sad that the new Museum
was not built out there, away from dust and traffic, where
things could have been shown out of doors and under open
porticoes, and where there would have been ample room for
the workshops and stores which were forgotten in the planning
of the pretentious edifice in Kasr el Nil. The present Museum
was opened in 1902, but owing to constructional defects, has
been almost constantly under repair ever since ; now, large
as it is, an extension has become urgently needed, which
will fill up much of the scanty space surrounding it.

Egypt has been very generous to foreign diggers in comparison with Italy, Greece, or Turkey, where all finds are considered
the property of the country. In Egypt the law, up to now,
has been that the Government had the right to half and the
excavator to half—except in the Valley of the Tombs of the
Kings, at Thebes, where a special arrangement was made.
This law has as a rule been liberally interpreted, the Egyptian
Museum desiring rather to acquire a few things of good quality
than to accumulate a mass of duplicates.

This Museum differs from most others in that everything in it belongs to ancient Egypt, whereas, everywhere else, the Egyptian collection is only one department of an assemblage of relics of all ages and from all parts of the world. So, in a sense, it is easier to see, but, on the other hand, hardly anyone comes to it with any previous knowledge of the subject, and it contains such a bewildering variety of styles and periods, so many objects of industrial, social and artistic interest dating from any part of the four thousand years of Egyptian history, that it is hopeless to learn much about it without some reading and a great number of visits.

It has been my lot to show it for the first time to many different people and I have been much interested to see the way in which they were affected by it. I think the most enjoyable people to go round with are artists, who are able to see a beautiful thing, however unfamiliar it may be. They rarely fail to point out something fresh and unobserved before. But those who know about any craft or industry are generally easy to interest also. Egypt saw the beginning of so many things. Jewellers will look at the technique of the gold work, weavers and embroiderers will ponder over the fine linen or the model looms, a yachtsman will enjoy working out the way the Middle Empire boats were rigged, a carpenter will identify the uses of tools, and so on indefinitely. It only wants time for most people to appreciate the great stores offered to them, except, indeed, the not inconsiderable proportion who are not historically minded and to whom things so old and so remote have little appeal. Even they, oddly enough, are often rather fascinated by the mummies.

It is somewhat of a question how much and what sort of interest is felt by the numerous Egyptian visitors who go over the Museum. The obvious answer would seem to be that they take the same kind of interest as everybody else, with the additional attraction, in their case, that they are looking at relics of their own past greatness. But it is hardly so simple as that. So much in this country is bound up with magical beliefs that it is always difficult to be sure that one is not coming up against them. A few years ago, there is

no doubt that all the Egyptian women who went to the
Museum, went from the sole motive of a desire to increase
their families, for it is a matter of universal knowledge that
there is no better specific for inducing fertility than looking at
antiquities, and how could one get a finer chance than to see
such a lot of them together ? I hesitate to say that this
motive is as general as formerly, for education has advanced
and family life of a more western type is becoming much
more frequent. Probably some of the daintily dressed little
ladies whom we see going about with their husbands and
children, simply look on the place as giving them a pleasant
outing and may even feel some curiosity about Tutankh-
amen. But one is never sure.

It is hardly surprising that, as a people, the Egyptians are
only beginning to take any interest in their own very ancient
history. After all, their background of Islam covers as
many centuries as does the whole history of most European
countries ; besides, the past of ancient Egypt is so remote
that it really means no more to the native of one country than
of another. What makes it so precious is the ever-growing
desire in all of us to get back to the beginnings, and it is
devoutly to be hoped that Egypt will rise to the wide vision
of her civilization as a world possession, of which she is the
appointed guardian.

I do not think that many people are prepared for the great
art that awaits them. The best of the Old Empire statues are
very great art indeed and the Cairo Museum has by far the
finest collection of these ; thanks, of course, to Mariette's early
finds. They were made as portraits, but not portraits for the
living to look at : rather as an extension of personality in
the next world, where, in some strange way, they were to
help the dead man to a continuance of life. They are very
life-like, and have been much praised as faithful portraits,
which, I suppose, they were, but surely, they are much more
than that.

Where the Greeks deliberately sacrificed individual character
and sought for the ideal type, the Egyptians, long before, had
tried to raise the individual, in dignity, vigour and repose,

PLATE II

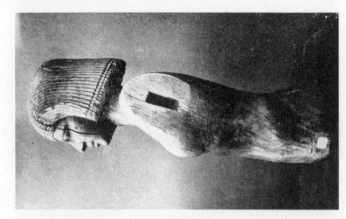

WOODEN FEMALE FIGURE

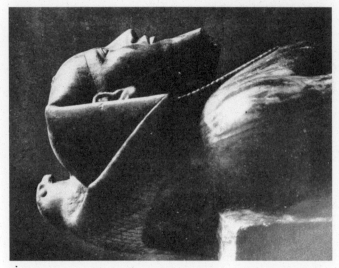

HEAD OF DIORITE STATUE OF CHEPHREN
(FOURTH DYNASTY)

until they attained an ideal of their own. Take the basalt
statue of Chephren, which once stood in the Valley Temple
of his pyramid (Plate II, 1). Can we think of it merely as a
portrait of the king to be set up as a piece of decoration ?
Is it not rather the figure of a god, majestic and imperturbable,
whom future ages will worship ? And the painted limestone
statues of Rahotep and Nefert, do they not show forth eternal
youth, complacent wedlock, unquestioned aristocracy, rather
than simple likenesses of the General of troops, Rahotep and
the Lady of the Court, Nefert ?

The technique of all these statues is astonishingly fine,
whatever be the material employed, from the hard diorite of
Chephren, the alabaster and slate of Mycerinus, the painted
limestone that most private people used, down to the wood of
the " Sheikh el Beled " and his wife (Plate II, 2) and, a little
later, the copper of King Pepy. It seems wonderful that even
a plain bit of wood should have survived for 5,000 years, but,
that carved wood should still show subtle, beautiful modelling
as in the statues of the Sheikh el Beled and the slender little
half-length of his wife, is a marvel only made possible by the
dry warm sand that covered them for so long. What will
be the life of these things, now they are shown to the world ?
It is a terrible thought that this generation may be using up
these unique, irreplaceable works of art. For Museums are
not houses of eternity, like the tombs. Not by any means.

I do not think that Egypt ever again reached the level of
the Old Empire ; the splendid dignity and simplicity of the
early days was never equalled, but there are some things of
an even more ancient date, which have the special interest
that they give us a glimpse of the beginnings. Up to about
thirty years ago, these Old Empire statues, the Pyramids
and the Sakkara tombs were accounted to be the very dawn
of history, and it was thought almost heretical to say that
art never could have leapt into being so full-grown and that
there must have been a long archaic period preceding them.
But it only needed more careful methods of digging to find
plenty of evidence for this prehistoric age and its archæology
is now comparatively well known. Most of the objects from

this remote antiquity are small and insignificant-looking, but a problem hangs about one famous group in the Museum, which may be found to date from this period.

Less beautiful than the Fourth Dynasty statues, but equally fine in workmanship, are the large figures in black granite, known as the Tanis statues. They seem to stand alone in art ; there is nothing like them, but recent discoveries at Sakkara lend support to the view that these black statues are even older than the Old Empire and that they may be relics of the vanished archaic art of northern Egypt. The type of face with its high cheek-bones and full lips, is strikingly like the statue of Neterhet, the builder of the Step Pyramid. Excavations are being carried on at present which are revealing a style of building that is very beautiful, but totally different from what is known at Giza and other places of the Fourth Dynasty art. It is too early to make any very definite statements about this astonishing discovery of objects of such high antiquity, but it certainly throws even farther back the beginning of great art in the world.

Anyone who is interested in the development of ancient art, will find some time well spent in looking over the ivories, flints and slates, the pottery and the beautiful stone vases in the prehistoric room, but for most people, it is better to see fine objects and be thankful, without questioning as to how they came into being, and such will do more wisely to concentrate themselves on the sculptures and on the furniture and jewellery.

Even the Fourth and Fifth Dynasty art was not all good ; many of the limestone figures lack life and grace, and must have been turned out mechanically, according to the type required ; some by skilful craftsmen, others, it would seem, by unpretending masons. The whole level declined a little before the collapse of the Old Empire, when darkness falls over the land for centuries. When Egypt gradually emerged again into the light, it was with a changed government, and many changed customs, though always the reverence for the dead and the hope of a future life persisted. In this Middle Empire civilization rose very high ; it was the classic period

in literature, and some will have it that it was the climax of
Art as well, but judging from what has come down to us, it
cannot be said that the sculptures approach those of the Old
Empire. The Middle Empire jewellery does, however, stand
out as being better than any other, and here again, the
Museum of Cairo is pre-eminent. The ancient robbers overlooked one or two boxfuls of jewellery hidden in the passages
of one of the Dahshur pyramids, and their contents have
filled two cases in the Cairo Museum which are a pure joy to
behold.

To this period belong also the wooden models of domestic
scenes ; extremely attractive things and very valuable for
archæology. There are a few bits of sculpture, too ; enough
to show us how very good their best must have been.

After the glorious Middle Empire, Egypt was plunged in
chaos again, but rose to her greatest heights of power under
the Eighteenth Dynasty, about 1500 B.C. From that date
onwards Egypt could draw largely on her neighbours for
luxuries, both by trade and tribute. Egyptian artists enjoyed
themselves painting all the new things that came in ; horses,
which had not long been introduced, lions and giraffes which
were brought from the Sudan for the royal gardens ; dresses,
embroideries and vases from Syria and the islands. So,
though the old conventions went on, there is a great deal more
variety in the scenes than there was formerly. One has to
see Luxor to realize this fully, but there is a good deal in the
Cairo Museum and some charming paintings in the British
Museum which illustrate this very well. The racial types
are always excellently done.

Foreign influence grew as time went on, though for a long
while the aims of artistic presentment were not altered. It
was beautiful decoration, very skilfully done, intended either
to glorify the king, or to procure a more varied and entertaining life in the next world for his loyal subjects. The
finest of the statues, like the small one of Thothmes III in
black basalt, are so refined and delicate in workmanship that
they carry our minds to Greece to find a parallel to them ;
but it is always the representation of youth and vigour, self-

satisfied and complete. Then a change came which was ushered in by one of the most interesting epochs in Egyptian history. This was Tell el Amarna, which, of late years, has become so fatally familiar a word. The character and physique of Akhenaten have been discussed by hundreds of people who neither know how little can be known of him, nor what that little is. And, as for his son-in-law, Tutankh-amen, whose name has suddenly flashed out from the dim past and dazzled the world, what can one say about him that will not fall flat and dead after all that has been said and written ? But if one is to write of Egyptian art at all, one must write of Tell el Amarna, for it is a page by itself and of immense importance. Let us leave to others the speculations of history and romance and stick to solid facts, the " chiels that winna ding," the sculptures and paintings and furniture that are there to be seen, and take them on their merits.

There we see the change of aims and ideals that had come over Egyptian art. I have said before that the dignity and simplicity of the Old Empire sculptures was never again reached ; certainly Tell el Amarna never equalled it—but then, it was trying after something different. What that something was, is best expressed in a few lines from Browning's " Old Pictures in Florence," when he is setting forth the difference he felt between the art of Greece and that of mediæval Italy.

> " To cries of ' Greek art, what more wish you ? '
> Replied, ' To become now self-acquainters,
> And paint man *man*, whatever the issue
> Make new hopes shine through the flesh they fray. . . .
> To bring the invisible full into play ! ' "

This is the inspiration of Tell el Amarna, and it is the solitary moment in the story of the ancient world when Art turned from its great traditions of beauty and proportion of body and tried to show the soul within. Can anyone look at the Nefertiti head and not feel that it transcends physical beauty : that it hardly matters whether she was or was not a beautiful woman in the accepted sense of the perfection of bodily form (Frontispiece) ? There never can have been many

masterpieces like this : in Cairo there are only a few little
heads that are worthy of comparison with it. But there is
enough to form an opinion.

The finest of the three heads of the king, on his Canopic
jars, is, to my thinking, one of the most lovely things in the
museum, but there are also in the case devoted to the Tell
el Amarna objects in the Eighteenth Dynasty room, several
small pieces which are exquisitely modelled and full of senti-
ment and sweetness. The grotesque shape of most of the
heads is disturbing, but perhaps may be explained by the
fact that all these pieces came from a sculptor's studio and
that many are unfinished. Such a head-dress as that worn
by Nefertiti might be made of gold and inlay and have been
set on the heads of the little princesses much in the same
way. But unfortunately this peculiarity, and the strange
shapes of some of the figures are enough to discourage many
people from looking more closely at these charming and
beautiful things. Perhaps Akhenaten had some physical
deformity which his love of truth and his revolt against con-
vention caused him to insist on his artists emphasizing. That
might have been safe in the hands of the very best, but it was
very easy to lapse into caricature. It is often put forward,
by way of accounting for Akhenaten's revolution, that he
must have been an epileptic, with an ill-formed body which
reacted on his mind ; that the artistic style of his period was
an effort by obsequious artists to make his deformity into a
new standard of beauty : that, at best, he was a dreamy
weakling, who let a great empire slip away, while he was
building temples to a fantastic worship. It is too far away to
know what really happened, but we may venture to doubt
whether, in art, such motives could ever have produced anything except caricature ; whether literature, under such an
influence, could ever have risen to pure poetry, as the Hymn
to the Aten undoubtedly is. If we read the Hymn and look
at the sculpture, it is simply impossible not to feel a lofty
and noble inspiration behind them.

How long it would have been practicable for any king to
have held Syria and Palestine as parts of the Egyptian Empire

it is hard to say, and it does not seem to matter very much. But it has mattered a great deal to the world, that Tell el Amarna, for one brief moment, did touch the heights. How much more than that Egypt should have kept her grip on Syria for a generation or two longer, and that her temples should have been even fuller than they are of the praises of Amen Ra !

It is well to have given this little amount of consideration to the art of Tell el Amarna, before approaching the tremendous find of the last three years, for in this way it may be possible, even at this early date, to give some kind of critical appreciation of the objects from the tomb of Tutankhamen which are already shown in the Museum.

I was in England at the time of the discovery of the tomb, so had not the good fortune to be present at the opening, but I can perfectly realize the immense excitement and enthusiasm which were roused by the spectacle of such treasure. The amount of it is overpowering. As I write, after more than two years, there is still a great deal to be brought out of the tomb ; the mummy has still to be unwrapped and stores of unopened boxes and large quantities of funerary furniture have to be examined. In variety and splendour there has never been anything like it. In the highest class of artistic excellence, I think most critics agree that it is just a little past the best. There is nothing that will rank as sculpture along with the very best of the generation before, and the richest pieces of furniture tend to be over-gorgeous and flamboyant, rather than graceful in line. But this is only true of the more magnificent pieces, such as the throne and the alabaster vases ; the great mass of the furniture is very fine, and the wooden figures of the king, the statues, the so-called " mannequin " and the ushabtiu statuettes are delightful bits of characteristic Tell el Amarna work.

The alabasters are real *tours de force* and are, I must admit, far more beautiful in reality than I thought they could be when I first saw the newspaper illustrations of them ; but why make such things of alabaster at all ? One or two of the less ornate are, indeed, exquisite pieces ; one in particu-

PLATE III

HEAD OF GRANITE STATUE OF THE GOD KHONSU
(NINETEENTH DYNASTY)

lar, which appears to have been made as a lamp, the design only being brought out when a light is placed inside, is a novel and charming idea. The great chair, or throne, is also a marvellous bit of work, with the inlaid figures of wonderfully modelled glaze on a gilt and jewelled background—but how much more beautiful is the other large chair, which is of plain dark wood and of simple but delicate design.

The workmanship is all extraordinarily fine ; the detail on the small ivory and wood carvings, the fastenings of boxes, the glaze modelling, all repay long and careful study and place the whole find in a class by itself as archæological material. There never has been anything like it and it may be that the greatest interest is yet to come, for the mummy of the king may have the royal robes and jewellery still untouched. Of all the objects now shown, I like most the chariots and the walking-sticks. The chariots are in pieces, as they were found, for there was no room in the tomb, as there is not room in the Museum until a special annexe has been built, to show them complete. But all the pieces are there, and the detail on the " aprons " of the chariots is most interesting. The walking-sticks are exquisite things ; the handles formed of figures of Asiatic and negro captives, sometimes singly, sometimes tied together. The tiny faces of the Asiatics are of toned ivory with hair, beards and eyebrows black, and a real expression of suffering upon some of the wrinkled brows. The negroes are of ebony ; also beautifully modelled.

The Tell el Amarna influence was still very strong for some time after the return to Thebes. It would be more correct to say that it was strong artistically, for in religion the reaction was violent and very rapid. Some of the most splendid buildings in the country date from the Nineteenth Dynasty, soon after the return to the worship of Amen, and they are all temples to his glory. These must, of course, be seen in place, but in the Museum there is a beautiful statue, dating from the time soon after the reaction, which shows how strong the inspiration of Tell el Amarna still was. This is a figure of the god Khonsu, the child god of the Amen triad (Plate III).

5

But we can see, only too plainly, as we pass through the later rooms, how, under the deadening conventionality imposed by the restored conditions, sculpture grew steadily more and more lifeless and mechanical. Art was only free to move in directions hitherto little heeded, like portraits, plain, unidealized portraits, which were very well done in the Saitic period, about 600 B.C. Small bronzes, too, were extremely charming in these later ages of Egyptian art, and the Museum has a fine collection of these. Other small objects are interesting, but to begin a description of any of these classes of things would be to write a catalogue *raisonné* ; there is so much that is good, so little that is outstanding.

There was a sort of Renaissance in the Saitic period. A good deal of restoration was carried on at the pyramids and the worship of the ancient kings was revived. Some reliefs in the Museum show this " archaistic " treatment and are curious and pleasing, but no one could mistake them for the Old Empire decoration which they imitate.

Of good Greek pieces there are a very few, but the remainder and all the Roman sculptures are rather undistinguished.

With the rise of Christianity the end came, for when Egypt turned her back on the old faiths, she put away along with them the writing that she had so long before given to the world and every representation of anything in heaven or in earth that had been used either as ornament or as written signs. She would have no more of such heathen symbols, and so forsook an art that had been very great and that was absolutely her own, for a foreign art and a lesser one, yet still an art that is not to be despised. Its inspiration is Byzantine, but Egypt gave it a special character and the interest of Coptic architecture and Coptic ornament to all students of early Christianity is great and is increasing.

But the most remarkable thing is the completeness of the break between old and new. Ancient Egyptian art rose and fell, varied its styles with varying epochs, was influenced by the art of other countries, but it was continuous. Coptic art, once started in Egypt, went on steadily and, when the Arab invasion came was not much affected by it. The Arabs of the desert brought no art with them, but they made their Christian subjects work for them, and the Coptic designs in stone and wood and glass adapted themselves so well to the complicated tracery of Arab ornament, that in the smaller artistic objects, there is no determining a time when we can say " This is Coptic " and " This again, is Arab." From the introduction of Christianity to the present day there are many differences, but there is continuity, as there was in the ancient art. The great gulf is fixed back in the fourth century between paganism and Christianity.

CHAPTER V

THE COPTIC CHURCH

" The church which is at Babylon saluteth you and so doth Marcus my son."

I DO not think that many people realize that these words almost certainly mean that the First Epistle of Peter was written from Old Cairo. Some will have it that Peter meant that he was at Rome and used the expression " Babylon " as a sort of cryptogram which would be understood by fellow-Christians. But, though it was natural that " Babylon " should be taken as a symbol for Rome in a book like the Revelation, it is surely more likely that a person, writing an ordinary letter, with messages in it, should call a place by its own name. Babylon of Mesopotamia had fallen into obscurity by that time, but Babylon of Egypt was, next to Alexandria, the largest Roman garrison in Egypt and a town of considerable size. It does not seem a straining of probabilities to suppose that Peter visited it on a missionary journey and that he left Mark there permanently. For, although no tradition links the church of Egypt up to St. Peter, that which looks back to Mark as the first bishop is very strong indeed and is generally accepted.

Evidently, according to all records, Egypt was very early Christianized. The philosophers of Alexandria had open minds for the discussion of all religious problems and discovered, in the new religion, a re-statement of many of the ideas which already prevailed among them. There seems no doubt that the doctrines of Christianity were considerably modified by this contact with Hellenistic philosophy, but on this slippery ground I dare not tread. The speculations which formed the chief intellectual interest of the world in these early centuries are so far removed from modern thought as to be incomprehensible to anyone not soaked in the literature of the period, and, so far as I know, there is no book which presents them in an intelligible way.

What we can be sure of is that Egypt had a large Christian population and many churches before the time of Diocletian, but his persecution was so thorough that there is very little of a material kind remaining to show how or where these churches were built. This persecution impressed the Christians of Egypt so deeply that to this day they date their era, not from the birth of Our Lord, but from the accession of Diocletian in A.D. 284, a somewhat gloomy way of reckoning time. The test to which suspected Christians were subjected was whether they would sacrifice to the statue of the Emperor. It is curious to read, among the papyri found in the Fayum towns, many certificates which had been granted to show that so and so had duly sacrificed and burnt incense, and also, to find accusations against certain magistrates of having taken bakshish and given such certificates without insisting on the ceremony.

After Diocletian abdicated in A.D. 303, the persecution died down, but the doleful beginning is only too true an indication of the subsequent history of the Coptic Church. For a couple of centuries there was a period of prosperity though not of rest, for the fight between Arius and Athanasius raged furiously, and the great bishop was no less than five times expelled from the see of Alexandria and driven east and west. His longest and most dangerous exile was mostly spent in Egypt, in hiding. He was harboured and protected by faithful adherents in town and country, but especially by the hermits of the Thebaid.

Egypt was the early home of asceticism and the cells of these lonely saints are to be found far and wide along the desert edge and amongst the ancient tombs. Too often do we see on the Sheikh Abdel Gurneh hill, a bit of beautiful Eighteenth Dynasty painting wilfully defaced as heathenish and a cross splashed on above it in heavy red paint. Besides these solitary anchorites, there were communities where groups of them were gathered round the central figure of a holy saint. It was in this way that monasticism arose, and it is not surprising that it should first have taken shape in Egypt, for the idea was already there. Among the strange flowerings of late Egyptian religion when mingled with Alexandrian philosophy, there appears to have been a marked movement towards renunciation of the world and a life of purity and austerity. One such community was, at all events, settled on the desert west of Alexandria, and there are allusions to others. So Christianity had only to take over an idea already familiar to the higher minds of the time, and this helps us to understand the very early rise of religious houses in Egypt. Some of these have lasted on from the beginning to the present day. In the Wady Natron, at Sohag and at the remote Monastery of SS. Anthony and Paul east of Beni Suef, the monks still live by their ancient rule. But most of the monasteries are in ruins. A very fine one was excavated some years ago at Sakkara by my husband. It was dedicated to Jeremias ; not the prophet, but an Egyptian saint who lived about A.D. 500, and was the first abbot of the community. The place is thus dated to the time of Justinian, contemporary with San Vitale at Ravenna and St. Sophia at Constantinople. The artistic resemblances are striking. The stone capitals and friezes from the Church of St. Jeremias are now in Cairo Museum and are splendid examples of Coptic art. A good many belong to the best period and must have been made directly under Byzantine sculptors, but there is some deterioration of style as time went on. The place did not last more than two and a half centuries, and probably, after the Muslim conquest, its exposed situation rendered it very liable to attack.

The church had originally been built with external orna- ment ; friezes of vine or acanthus pattern decorated the whole length of it above the windows, and there were beautifully carved and extremely ornate doorways. But later, for protection from the constant danger of destruction by Muslim adversaries, these fine stones were taken down and carefully built up into massive brick walls, with the carved face inwards.

The monks' cells were rather pleasantly arranged. There were little suites for each man ; an oratory, a small sleeping place and an open veranda. The oratory was often decorated with paintings, some good, but here, as elsewhere, the style degenerated as time went on. Eventually, the place seems to have become too dangerous and the library with all the portable church furniture was moved to some safer abode.

Before A.D. 1000 it was deserted and in ruins. The latest inscription found on the walls was a graffito in a very early Arabic script, testifying that " there is no god but Allah and that Mohammed is the apostle of Allah."

In less dangerous places the churches and monasteries went steadily on, sometimes struggling, sometimes flourishing, but by that time, entirely cut off from communion with the sister churches in Europe.

The Egyptians, in adopting Christianity did it with extraordinary fervour. Their eagerness to get rid of all the old heathen symbols as well as the heathen worship, made them set aside their ancient art as completely as they possibly could. Their new art, as well as their script, was imported from Byzantium. The church architecture is Byzantine, with differences. But I am inclined to think that the differences were caused by circumstances rather than intention. Some of the churches at Old Cairo were founded as early as the fourth or fifth century, but they have all been altered and largely rebuilt since then.

The distinguishing feature of Coptic churches and monasteries as we see them to-day is that, when they stand open to view, out on the desert, they are like military forts ; when they are in the town, they are hidden away among clusters of surrounding buildings. The reason is the same for both : security. In the open, when they could not be concealed, they were defended by massive walls, as at the White Monastery at Sohag ; or by a keep and drawbridge, as at some of the monasteries in the Wady Natron. In Old Cairo the churches are behind blank walls in tortuous lanes, with only a low side entrance to give access to the rich interior. The oldest of the churches were built within the enclosure of the Roman fortress, which, in its present form, was the work of Trajan. Above one of the towers of this fort is the Greek church of St. George, while between the two bastions of the water gate is the Cathedral church of the Copts, dedicated to the Virgin, but generally known as " El Mu' allaka "— the " hanging," from its lofty position above the Roman wall.

The best authority for these churches and the other Christian monuments is Butler's " Ancient Coptic Churches of Egypt," but the Old Cairo churches are now much better kept and easier to see than they were when Butler wrote. Reference to this book shows what the original church of El Mu' allaka looked like, but without that it is rather difficult to understand, for it has suffered much both from plunderers and from ancient restorers. A fine pulpit remains, of marble and mosaic, very like the Saracenic pulpits in some churches in South Italy, where the ornament is known as " Cosmato work." There is also some beautiful woodwork, but the paintings are neither very old nor very interesting.

Round the garden court of the church a Museum of Coptic art has lately been arranged through the exertions of Marcus Pasha Simaika. It is delightfully planned ; the building is modern, but has been designed to suit the exhibits. The wooden roofs have been saved from old houses that were falling into ruins, the windows have been covered with old mushrabia work, the floors are on different levels, and the whole effect of the old woodwork and the whitewashed walls is extremely pleasant. The secular objects are, as is to be expected, indistinguishable from similar objects in the Arab Museum. For it must be remembered that the Arab invaders and the first converts to Islam were few in number, compared with the mass of the population, so that the whole of the art and industry remained in Christian hands. Even after many centuries, when a large proportion of the Egyptians had become Mohammedan, they still retained great skill in handiwork, which was employed to the full by the rulers of the country, of whatever race they might be. The Copts had their churches and their paintings long before the Arab conquest, and these were anathema to the true believers, but their mosaic work, carved ivory and elaborate screens of wood, with ivory and ebony inlay, were singularly well adapted for the decoration of Muslim buildings, either mosques or private houses.

The Church of Abu Sergeh, which most visitors go to see, is within the fortress and bears out what has been said about the curious unobtrusiveness of these churches. Its crypt is very ancient ; it is the traditional dwelling-place of the Holy Family, during their sojourn in Egypt. The tradition appears to be extremely old ; at all events, the style of the little chapel and the very low level at which it is built, make it fairly certain that it is considerably older than the church above it. It may well be that it was there before the time of Diocletian and escaped the general destruction of the churches which was carried out by his orders. It must be one of the oldest sanctuaries of Christendom. Upstairs, in the church, are some beautiful things ; especially to be noted is the " tribune " which is a feature of Coptic churches. Tiers of marble steps surround the central apse. These were for the church dignitaries and the Chair of the patriarch is in the middle, so that he and the priests who were not officiating, looked down on the altar from behind. This very ancient arrangement is to be seen in some Western Churches, Torcello, Ravenna and probably others.

The Church of Abu Seyfen, which lies outside the fortress, near the mosque of Amr, is perhaps the most attractive of all, as it has not been so much damaged in the past. It is not so old as the two just described, at least it seems to have been entirely rebuilt in the tenth century, in the time of the unorthodox Fatimite caliphs, when the Christians were having one of their occasional respites from persecution and were able to devote time and money to the repair of their own religious buildings. Like the others, it is so hidden away among the houses that it is only from some points that it is possible to catch sight of its inconspicuous little dome and the entrance is difficult to find. Abu Seyfen is really a beautiful church, with a very fine pulpit, like the one in El Mu' allaka, but better (Plate IV) ; with good paintings, and the usual elaborate screen made of wood and ivory dovetailed together without nails ; exactly the same work as we see in the doors and " mimbars " of mosques. The church is dedicated to St. Mercurius, popularly called Abu Seyfen—the possessor of two swords—to show what a great warrior he was. He was certainly a soldier, but the legend which makes him the slayer of Julian the Apostate is not easy to account for. The picture of him, riding over Julian's prostrate figure and brandishing his two swords, is quite a lively piece of work. These paintings are, at best, more curious than beautiful, but up to the fifteenth or sixteenth century they have some merit ; there is little to be said for anything that has been done since. Two or three more churches are described by Butler, all of the same type, having once been very rich, but, in spite of careful concealment, all having suffered much from plunder and neglect. All of them had, and most still have, Deirs or convents attached to them, in which a large part of the outside population sheltered in times of stress and trouble.

At Old Cairo one ought to think of the Roman fortress, as well as of the Coptic churches. It is interesting to go through the gate below the church of El Mu' allaka, which was the original entrance. The massive towers and the ornament over the gateway are in curious contrast with the Christian building above, and are one of the few pieces of fine Roman work in Egypt. When Amr ibn el Asy and his Arab followers entered the place in triumph, one wonders whether they were more impressed by the colossal masonry of the gate, with its marble pillars and the Imperial statues standing in its niches, or by the rich and sombre detail of the Cathedral church above.

The Arabs brought no art or industry with them. The account of the first mosque of Egypt, which was built by Amr just outside the walls of Babylon, shows the simple austerity of the early Muslims who had descended from the Arabian deserts into the fertile and luxurious land,

PLATE IV

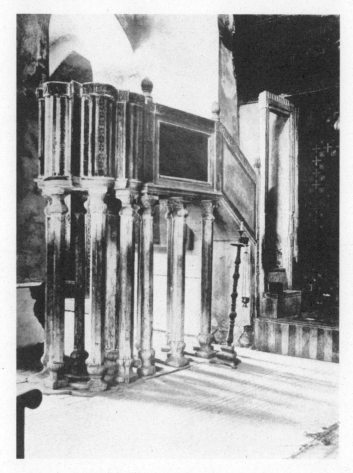

PULPIT IN CHURCH OF ABU SEYFÊN, OLD CAIRO (circ. 1000 A.D.)

A mosque still stands upon the site, but it has nothing remaining of the original building, not even the plan.

Amr's mosque is said to have been

" a simple oblong room, 28 metres long by 17 broad ; the low roof, no doubt, supported by a few columns . . . the walls probably of baked, but very possibly of unbaked, bricks, and unplastered ; the floor pebble strewn, the light probably supplied, as in the great colonnade at the present day, through square apertures in the roof. It possessed no minaret, nor other attractive outside feature ; no niche, nor any other internal decoration. In this humble building the conqueror of Egypt, as the caliph's representative, led the public prayers and preached the sermon, standing on the floor, for the caliph forbade the elevation of a pulpit. Amr's own house was opposite the entrance of the mosque."

Amr seems to have been something of a poet, as well as a soldier and an administrator. The following quotation from Butler's " Arab Conquest of Egypt " embodies the report on the country which he sent to the Caliph of Mecca, and, in its vivid, imaginative language, shows the effect of the rich, well-watered land with its seemingly docile people, upon the wild sons of the desert.

Butler says :

" The description of Egypt gives an interesting glimpse of Amr, both as poet and statesman. It was in rhymed prose and ran as follows : ' Know, O Commander of the Faithful, that Egypt is a dusty city and green tree. Its length is a month, and its breadth ten days. The Nile traces a line through its midst : blessed are its early morning voyages and its travels at eventide. It has its season for rising and for falling, according to the course of the sun and the moon. It causes milk to flow, and brings cattle in abundance. When the springs and fountains of the land are loosened, it rolls its swelling and sounding waters till the fields are flooded on both sides. Then there is no escaping from village to village save in little boats and frail skiffs, and shallops light as fancy or the evening mists. After the river has risen to its full measure, it sinks back again to its former level. Moreover the people, who are devout in worship, and are our protected allies, have learnt to plough the earth well and truly and to hasten the seedtime, trusting that the Most High will give the increase and will grant the fruit of their labour, though the labour is light. So the crop is grown and streams of water bring on the harvest, as moisture from beneath gives nourishment. At one time Egypt is a white pearl ; then golden amber ; then a green emerald ; then an embroidery of many colours.

" ' Blessed be God, because it has pleased him to bestow benefits upon this land, to give it increase, and so to establish the inhabitants in their country that no sound of complaint is heard from the people to their ruler ; that the land tax is not demanded before its due season ; and that a third of the revenue is spent on bridges and sluice gates. If the governors continue to act thus, the revenue will be doubled and God will reconcile the different religions and the variety of worldly interests.' "

Amr's gratitude to God, on behalf of Egypt, for the benefits conferred on her by Muslim rule, would hardly have been shared by the Egyptian people, though perhaps the terms he agreed to were fairly well kept for a time. These were that the Christians should remain undisturbed in the possession of their churches and the practice of their religion, but that they should pay a certain tribute, from which those who accepted Islam were exempt. But this did not last long, although active persecution was only intermittent. As centuries passed, more and more of the population gradually went over, although, in Upper Egypt and Nubia the change only came about comparatively recently. The surprising thing is that the process was so slow, and that the Coptic church, totally cut off, as it was, from all other Christians, and having suffered long and terrible oppression, should still reckon, as it does, so large and influential a minority of the Egyptian people among its members.

CHAPTER VI

THE CITADEL OF CAIRO

AN infant of days beside the Pyramids, of hoary antiquity compared with the modern town, the Citadel is the great expression of mediæval Cairo, the home and the fortress of the rulers of Egypt. It is not by any means the oldest building of Cairo ; it is not, by a century or so, as old as parts of the walls and some of the gates, but its erection marked a new departure in the growth of the place. The Citadel was the Acropolis, the possession of which has always denoted the supremacy over Egypt. It crowns a rocky promontory that juts out from the precipitous cliffs of the Mokattam hills, where the Arabian desert breaks sheer down to the Nile valley, and, from its massive towers and bastions, the view over the wide-spreading Delta and the narrow, green ribbon of Upper Egypt winding among sandy wastes, with the domes and minarets of the town close under-neath, is extremely imposing and beautiful.

It is a very famous view and has been described by many writers, but in addition to its magnificence, it has the advantage of giving a splendid starting-point for a survey of the history and development of the town of Cairo. It illustrates a principle which is of general application to Egyptian towns, namely, the tendency to extend northwards ; to reach out for more of the blessed north wind than the earlier quarters had. Turn south, to where the pyramids on their desert ridge overlook the valley. There was Memphis, an enormous place, which lasted for four thousand years and stretched for many miles along the Nile. When Memphis decayed, another city rose, some distance farther north and on the opposite

65

side of the river. This bore the strange name of Babylon and may have been founded by the Assyrian conquerors of Egypt in the sixth century before Christ. When the Romans came, this and not Memphis was the most important place they found and was chosen as the chief garrison for the interior of the country. When they in turn were driven out by the Arabs in the seventh century A.D., Amr ibn el Asy pitched his camp outside the fortress walls. The Arab town rose northwards and eastwards, towards the Mokattam hills, and was known as Fustat or Misr. Egypt was held as a province of the Caliphs, until, in A.D. 868, Ahmed ibn Tulun, a Turk or Turcoman by race, was appointed governor and was strong enough to render Egypt practically independent of Baghdad. He made a great enlargement of the town, extending it—northwards, of course—to where the big Place Rumeyla, just below the Citadel, now is. His palace is said to have been a marvel of beauty and luxury and was surrounded by magnificent gardens. The palace has long vanished, but the mosque that he built is one of the most remarkable in existence and is very prominent in the view from the Citadel.

Ibn Tulun's successors were overthrown, in A.D. 953, by an invasion from the west by the Fatimite Muslims, of whom more will be said in the chapter upon the mosques and Arab monuments. The victorious general, on the very night of his arrival, proceeded to lay the foundations of a new city for the new rulers. He was encamped about a mile to the north-east of Fustat, on the way to Heliopolis and there marked out his boundaries, which lie now under a busy and populous part of Cairo, more or less covering the quarter of the bazaars. The planet Mars was in the ascendant, and the new town was named in his honour, Elkahira; El Kahir being the Arabic form of Mars.

The Fatimite rulers lasted for about two centuries, and before the end of that period, the Crusading age had come, a new factor which was to affect Egypt considerably, though not to recover her to Christendom.

By the middle of the twelfth century the Western invaders had covered Palestine and Syria with castles and churches, a

Christian king was reigning in Jerusalem and this new Christian power had thrust a wedge between Muslim Damascus and Muslim Egypt.   But Damascus was orthodox and Egypt was Shi'ite and there was a temptation to both parties to intrigue against one another with the foreigner.   Egypt was rich, was weakened by misrule and likely to be a fairly easy prey.   The Christian leaders had begun to realize that without some source of supplies on which they could rely, it would be difficult to hold Jerusalem.   The enthusiasm that carried Godfrey of Bouillon and his followers to victory had died away and their successors were more concerned with carving out principalities for themselves or acquiring plunder to take back to Europe than with the protection of the holy sites.   In the campaigns and negotiations the Crusaders almost invariably kept worse faith than their Muslim adversaries, and the complication of this bit of history is appalling.   The tale of the successive wars and alliances between King Amalric of Jerusalem with Egypt on the one hand and Sultan Nur ed Din of Damascus on the other is quite out of our scope, but the upshot was that Amalric was at last seriously defeated in Egypt and a great number of Frankish prisoners were taken by Shirkuh, the general, who had been sent to the help of Egypt by Nur ed Din.   This time the armies of orthodox Islam had come to stay and they quietly dispossessed the old and feeble Fatimite caliph, though for some little time they acknowledged him as the legitimate ruler.

Shirkuh died after two years and was succeeded by his nephew Saladin in the anomalous position of deputy of an orthodox Sultan and Prime Minister of a Shi'ite caliph.   The two rulers were prayed for in the mosques, but when the old caliph was near his end, Saladin made the inevitable change and in 1171 the Abbasid caliph of Baghdad was proclaimed in Cairo.

Saladin at once began great alterations on the town of Cairo. He was accustomed to the Syrian towns, all of which had a citadel fortress, and his soldier's eye saw the possibilities of the site of Cairo. Before the days of cannon, the Mokattam hills dominated the town, and Saladin intended not only to build the Citadel on the projecting spur, but also to enclose the whole town with walls, making an immense circuit from the river, taking in the old Fatimite walls on the north, all the quarter where Tulun's buildings were, and round to Babylon on the south. Not very much of this large scheme was ever carried out, but during Saladin's eight years in Egypt he accomplished an astonishing amount. He built a great part of the Citadel and portions of the walls, and moreover, introduced a new style of architecture for the religious edifices, which will be described in a later chapter. His architect, or architects, are said to have come from Syria, but he employed the Frankish prisoners taken in the recent campaign, in the building of the Citadel and in digging out the great well for the water supply, which is 280 feet in depth with a winding slope down the first half, then a straight drop to the bottom. Lane Poole quotes from a Spanish traveller who visited Cairo in 1183 and saw the prisoners at work.

" Both the workmen whose forced labour is employed for building the Citadel and their overseers are Christian prisoners of war of the Franks : their number is so great as cannot be reckoned and but for them there would be no means of carrying out these works, for only they can support the toil and heavy labour of sawing the marble (*sic*), dressing the great blocks of stone, and of quarrying the fosse which encompasses the wall of the Citadel, which fosse is cut like a dish in the solid rock with crowbars, a wonder of wonders for ever."

Saladin's Citadel was divided, as it still is, into a northern and a southern enclosure. The southern, which contains the Well, the mosque of Nasr ibn Kalaun, the Bijou Palace, the mosque and many other buildings of Mehemet Aly, has been so much altered that nothing of the original plan is to be seen. The northern enclosure, however, is almost entirely surrounded by Saladin's walls (Plate V, 1). These have recently been explored by Captain Creswell, who has made an exhaustive publication of the Citadel fortifications and has been kind enough to show me the long internal galleries and the disposition of the towers, which were strengthened and enlarged

PLATE V

CITADEL OF CAIRO FROM THE DESERT. WALLS OF SALADIN

MAUSOLEUM OF SULTAN BARKUK

by Saladin's brother, El Adil. There were two gates : one facing the town and approached by a steep slope, all the way under fire from arrow slits in the walls. This gate, known as the Bab el Mudarrag or " Gate of the steps," bore an inscription which may still be read, recording the

"building of this splendid Citadel,—hard by Cairo the Guarded, on the terrace which joins use to beauty and space to strength, for those who seek the shelter of his power,—was ordered by our master the King Strong to aid, Honour of the World and the Faith, Conquest laden, Yusuf, son of Ayyub, Restorer of the Empire of the Caliph."

This gate is now built up behind the Bab el Gedid, which Mehemet Aly made as the entrance for his driving road. The other gate, Bab el Qarafa, was towards the desert, and was discovered quite lately, in the course of Captain Creswell's excavations. It was known from literature, but had totally disappeared under accumulations of sand and rubble.

Saladin never lived in the Citadel although he probably began the building of a palace on the spot where now is the Detention Barracks, and from which there is a glorious view over Cairo and the Delta.

Saladin has become a figure of romance in both East and West, and, for once, Romance seems hardly to have exaggerated. Loyal, brave, wise and temperate, he is the greatest man of his time and was admired and trusted at once by those of his own religion and by the roystering, slippery champions of the Crusades. He left Egypt to carry the arms of the Crescent through Palestine and to drive the Crusaders from Jerusalem, and the rest of his life was spent in the struggle. He drew largely on Egypt for supplies, but his chief reliance for fighting men was on his Turkish and Circassian slave troops, who, from this time onwards, play a great part in all Islamic countries and, very notably, in Egypt.

The term " Mamluk " means, literally, " a possession," but the word, which has passed into English as " Mameluke," became restricted in significance to a male white slave. Large numbers of these were raided or otherwise acquired in Turkes-

6

tan or Circassia, brought as boys to be trained to a military life and became a splendid body of soldiers. They composed the Sultan's bodyguard and must have had quarters provided for them in the Citadel from the very first.

Saladin had, before his death, attained to the supreme power in Palestine and Syria as well as in Egypt, and left his empire divided between his three sons, but the Egyptian sultan was not a vigorous sovereign and the reins of government were actually held by his uncle, Saladin's brother, El Adil Seph el Din, a very able man, well known to the Crusaders as Saphedin. Richàrd Cœur de Lion went so far as to propose a marriage between Saphedin and his sister, the princess of England, but the divergences of creed and customs were insurmountable. Saphedin was, however, extremely broad-minded and so was his son and successor Kamil, under whom there came about a curious rapprochement between East and West. This was very largely due to the Emperor Frederick II and the extraordinary Crusade, in which, though under the papal interdict at the time, he regained possession of the Holy City for Christendom. Frederick had no objections to the Muslims at all, and when Kamil asked his alliance against his brother the Sultan of Damascus, he was quite willing to negotiate. A treaty was signed between the two monarchs and friendly correspondence passed, until the toleration of the Sultan for his Christian allies and subjects gave rise to a hope in the Catholic Church that he might be contemplating a change of religion and they dispatched a saintly missionary to aid in his conversion. It may well be—and it is a strange thought—that St. Francis of Assisi preached in the palace of the Cairo Citadel before Saladin's nephew. Apparently his preaching remained without effect, but he was well received and sent safely back to Italy.

This dynasty of Saladin's family lasted until 1249, when the Seventh Crusade, headed by St. Louis of France, landed at Damietta.

The King of France, believing that the way to recover the Holy Sepulchre for Christendom, was to strike, not by Syria as heretofore, but through Egypt, had brought as much of

his army as he could muster along with him, but owing to
quarrels of his knights and storms by sea, the force was not
nearly so strong as he had reckoned it would be. And the
landing at Damietta was a great mistake, the more serious as
it was in the season of full flood and he had to work his way
along dykes and across canals, whereas, if he had attacked
Cairo from the north, up the Wady Tumilat and along the
desert edge, there might have been a chance of success, for
the Egyptians, on their side, were by no means in a good
case.

Their sultan, Salih Ayyub, was dying, the heir was far away
and the Mameluke leaders were fighting among themselves.
All this tale, from the French side, is fascinatingly told in
Joinville's chronicle; the manner in which he makes the character of the Christian king stand out from among his quar-
relling, drunken followers, has become a classic.

The Crusading army fought its way up to Mansura, and,
by that time, had anyone known it, the Sultan Salih Ayyub
lay dead in his tent in the midst of the Muslim camp. But
there was a woman there, Shegeret el Dur, once a slave,
who had borne him a son and so obtained her freedom and
some royal rights. She took command of the situation, in
concert with one or two faithful emirs; concealed the Sultan's
death from friends and foes, issued a daily bulletin of his
health and sent trays of delicate food to the tent where his
body lay. She used the Sultan's seal, the chief eunuch forged
his signature, and between them, all the needful orders were
given and a secret messenger was dispatched to recall the
absent heir Turanshah, who was in Mesopotamia.

The Crusaders gained a short-lived and dearly bought victory at Mansura, but when Turanshah arrived and took
command, he contrived to stop all supplies to the Frankish
army and refused peace negotiations. King Louis was
obliged to set out on a desperate retreat to Damietta, burning
his engines of war and relying on rapid and light going. But
the army was very sick and nearly starving; in no state to
march and at the same time withstand the attacking Saracens,
who harassed the rearguard. Finally, the King and nearly

all the French host were taken prisoners. A ransom was agreed on for a large sum of money and the surrender of Damietta, but just at that juncture, the new Sultan, Turan-shah, was murdered. The Mamelukes were very loath to let the captives go at any price, and, had it not been for Shegeret el Dur, who, to her eternal honour, insisted on keeping faith with the infidel, the saintly king, together with many nobles in whose veins was the best blood of France, would have ended their lives on the dreary Delta plain.

She was actually elected Sultan after this by the Mamelukes, who from now on were to be the holders and disposers of the Egyptian throne, but the anomaly of a woman ruler was too outrageous to the spirit of the age and the Caliph of Bagh-dad sent word to the emirs in Egypt that, if they had no *man* among them, he would send one. This hint was too strong not to be acted on, so Aybek, one of their number, was chosen to be the husband of Shegeret el Dur. She clung to the real power, however, very tenaciously ; all she wanted of Aybek was to do the fighting, while she took entire charge of the finance. Although she lived always on very bad terms with him, she could not stand the idea of a rival wife, and, when Aybek made overtures to marry a princess of Mosul, Shegeret el Dur had him murdered in his bath in the Citadel Palace. Although she had a party of protectors among the emirs there was not much competition for the vacant post of being her husband, and her position rapidly became perilous. Not long after Aybek's murder, she herself was dragged before a previous wife whom she had compelled Aybek to divorce, and was beaten to death by the clogs of the women slaves of her rival. Salih el Ayyub had been the last of Saladin's dynasty ; Shegeret el Dur was really the first of the Mamelukes, and this extraordinary succession of adventurers went on until the Turkish conquest in 1517. The race was always to the swift and the battle always to the strong ; Mameluke after Mameluke fought his way to power and kept it just so long as he was able to keep his rivals under.

The period is divided into two, the first called Turkish,

the second Circassian, but it really may be considered as continuous.

All these Mameluke rulers were brave fighters and none had any scruples, for they rose to power by violence and treachery and held it by terror, yet those who were strong enough to keep the mastery for a lengthened space of time were generally fairly just to their subjects.

And almost all of them were magnificent patrons of art and learning. It is amazing to think of the life in that blood-stained Citadel, with the cruel dungeons underneath that teemed with awful secrets, and the Palace above, where the Sultan and his emirs, dressed in marvellous robes and surrounded by objects of most delicate beauty, spent their days in the enjoyment of banqueting, music and poetry.

There was great wealth in the country. The Crusades had developed trade with the East, and some Italian towns, Venice of course pre-eminently, were doing an immense trade, a great deal of which came through Egypt. The merchandise that arrived by sea at Suez was carried by the canal which connected the Bitter Lakes with the Nile, and so down the river to Damietta, and it all paid customs dues to Egypt. Indeed, the revenue from this source was so large that the taxes from the Egyptian fellahin were of secondary importance. The land was divided into Mameluke fiefs and the Egyptians existed only to do the work for them, so it is difficult to know much about their condition, but the probabilities are that they all, even the Christians, had considerable intervals of rest from active oppression.

One of the first and most notable of the Mameluke sultans was El Daher Beybars, who was born somewhere between the Caspian and the Ural mountains ; a tall, strong man, but with one eye disfigured, which spoiled his price in the slave market, where he is said only to have fetched the equivalent of £20. He rose to be a highly successful general, and, as Sultan, extended the border of Egypt over most of the neighbouring countries. He became a legendary character and tales of his adventures and disguises were still circulating in Cairo in the nineteenth century.

Under him there was not only a system of posts connecting all parts of his empire, by means of which he sent out and received letters twice every week, but he had also a pigeon post, probably for more private correspondence. The pigeons were kept in cots at the Citadel and were trained to stop at regular stages. The end of Beybars was the usual one. He died of poison, a poison, it is said, prepared by him for another use.

Another eminent sultan was Kalaun, who actually founded a kind of dynasty, which lasted, with some interruptions, to the end of the Turkish period. He did a great deal of building in Cairo, though not much on the Citadel hill. His son Nasr, however, covered it with the finest buildings that have ever stood there, and he constructed the long aqueduct from the Nile to the Citadel hill, which is a very prominent feature of Cairo to this day. By his time, so many people lived in the fortress that the old well no longer gave an adequate supply and he had to have recourse to the river.

By all accounts his palace in the Citadel was magnificent ; the great hall, which was standing at the time of Napoleon's expedition, seems to have been most beautiful. It occupied part of the space that we now have to cross to reach the mosque of Mehemet Aly, who swept it and a good deal more of Nasr ibn el Kalaun's building away to make room for renovations. Nasr's mosque still stands, and, though it has suffered terribly from neglect and wilful damage, anyone who has seen something of Arab architecture will appreciate its fine, simple lines and the excellence of the perishing ornament that remains. Most unusual are the two tiled minarets, which are unique in Egypt and are supposed to be due to the influence of Nasr's wife, a Tartar princess. The Mongols had advanced far west by that time and Nasr was not the only Egyptian sultan who made political and matrimonial alliance with the Golden Horde.

During the Circassian period life went on much in the same way : sultan succeeded sultan if anything more quickly than before and the throne was even more unstable, but for a time, the great wealth, the luxury and the wonderful artistic achievements continued. During the sixteenth century, however, a change came over the world and Egypt began to decline, even as Venice was declining, and for the same reasons. First of these was the conquest of Constantinople by the Ottoman Turks, the overthrow of the Christian powers remaining in the Levant and the stoppage of all trade from that quarter; second and important for Egypt, the discovery of the route to the East round by the Cape of Good Hope. However, up to the time of the Turkish conquest in 1517, Cairo was very rich and building very splendid. The last of the Mameluke sultans, El Ghury, restored Nasr ibn el Kalaun's aqueduct to the Citadel and built a tomb for himself and a small but beautiful mosque down in the town.

But the blight of Turkish misrule crushed the art of Egypt, and the poverty induced by the falling off of the customs revenues rendered recovery hopeless. A mosque of the Turkish period built soon after the conquest, is in the Citadel and is worth going to see. It is a pleasing little edifice, but the contrast with the earlier building is very marked. As to the life and the government, there was not very much outward change. The place of the Mameluke troops in the Citadel was taken by the Janissaries, who were much the same sort of slave troops, without family ties and owing duty to no one but the Sultan.

The Mameluke nobles took refuge for a time in their country estates, but they came back again later, when the Turkish rule relaxed, and, throughout the eighteenth century they seem to have been fighting among themselves for the supreme power, under a loose allegiance to the Porte. One important addition to the Citadel that dates from this time is the Bab el Azab, which gives access from the Place Rumeyla to a narrow road leading up to the Bab el Mudarrag. This was the main entrance to the fortress, until Mehemet Aly made the driving road that now winds up the hill.

The old life of the Middle Ages was going on untouched by the West when Napoleon landed in Egypt in 1798 and defeated the Mameluke army on the other side of the Nile, in what is known as the Battle of the Pyramids, but which

actually took place at Embabeh. He took possession of
Cairo, but did not take up his quarters in the Citadel, where,
however, he built a monument that must not be left without
mention ; namely, the fort on the hill behind. It was erected
after a revolt by the Cairo people, which he repressed with
severity, but without much difficulty, for he had cannon
dragged up to the Mokattams and demonstrated that the
old Acropolis had become useless in modern warfare ; the
commanding site was helpless against the big guns posted
on the cliffs above.

Another achievement of Napoleon's was a peaceful one,
which has been of the utmost value to lovers of Egypt as well
as to historians. The young general had a real curiosity about
the mysterious country which had been shut off for so long
from Europe, and he attached to his staff, before leaving
France, a number of eminent scholars and men of science,
in order that they should report as fully as possible upon
every aspect of the country. Their labours are embodied in
the " Description de l'Egypte," a superb publication and a
monument of extraordinary industry on the part of its com-
pilers. From the " Description " we get a good idea of
what the Citadel was like in 1798, when the French took
possession.

The first building to be seen on reaching the top of the
hill was the Palace of Saladin ; a complete ruin, but
still marked by a few standing walls and columns. On
the other hand, the great hall or Diwan of Nasr ibn el
Kalaun was nearly perfect in its preservation and thirty-seven
splendid pillars were noted there, as well as many pieces of
painting and mosaic decoration. At the southern end of
the Citadel enclosure was the Palace of the Turkish governor,
now known as the Bijou Palace, one or two mosques of the
Turkish period, the Mint and other Government offices. The
castle was supplied with water by six well shafts, the most
important being the so-called " Well of Joseph " already
described. (I suppose this must mean that the aqueduct had
again fallen out of repair and that the direct supply from the
Nile was not available.)

The French also state that they found fourteen subterranean reservoirs, the largest of which lies underneath the entrance to the present Hospital and was large enough to contain a supply of water sufficient for ten thousand people for a year. Many dungeons and cellars cut in the rock were also examined, but probably Time failed the French explorers to plan them.

After Napoleon and his soldiers and savants had withdrawn from Egypt, the old, mediæval state of things returned for a while, but with a difference. Although the Mameluke emirs did not seem to have learned much from their defeat, they had had a hard knock, and the Turkish sultan seized the chance to revive the authority of the Porte. He sent a slave general, Khusrev, as his deputy. Khusrev occupied the Citadel, but the country belonged absolutely to the Mamelukes, and, as the revenue now depended entirely on agriculture, a fight for the possession of the land inevitably ensued. The Mamelukes were divided in their allegiance between two rival emirs, and, for the next few years, the state of the Egyptian inhabitants was perhaps more miserable than it had ever been throughout their long history. None of the three combatants was strong enough to get the better of the other two, and the distracted land offered every opportunity to any powerful outsider, who could throw the necessary force into the balance. And there was one ready and on the spot. Mehemet Aly, the beginning of whose career was described in the chapter on Alexandria, had stayed on in Egypt and was the very man fitted by character and circumstances to fish in these troubled waters. He played off the Mamelukes against each other and against Khusrev ; he had a band of brave Albanians ready to fight for anything he wanted, he was backed by the townspeople, who would have welcomed any change, and at last he wrung recognition from the Porte and gained a footing in Egypt. It was precarious at first, but, in 1806 a great mistake on the part of England was a great stroke of fortune for him. England was then at war with Turkey and sent a force to help the Mamelukes in Egypt, not at all realizing that now a really strong man was in power

there. The small body of English troops was badly beaten
and nearly five hundred English prisoners were marched up
to the Citadel, where other English soldiers had entered as
conquerors only five years before. These prisoners were
not at all badly treated, for the last thing Mehemet Aly wanted
was to bring a serious attack from England against him. His
aim was to pose as the champion of the Porte and the Defender
of Islam, and this he had been lucky enough to do. He set
earnestly to work, now that his position was more secure, to
get the country into better order, and, by 1810 by means of
heavy exactions from the peasants, he had made a good deal
of progress, but he was pulled up by a sudden menace from
the Porte. The Sultan, in the time-honoured Turkish way,
had grown suspicious of such a vigorous subordinate and
thought it would be well to get him out of the way in a manner
which would at once bring glory to Turkey and enable her
to renew her grip on Egypt, which was getting better worth
holding. So he ordered an expedition from Egypt against
the Wahhabis of Arabia. Mehemet Aly was obliged to agree,
but where was he to get the money for it ? The fellahin
were squeezed dry already ; any little more that could be
wrung out of them would hardly count towards the expense
of fitting out a large force by sea and land. There remained
the Mamelukes, who owned nearly all the land in Upper
Egypt and were still a danger, for, though they were keeping
quiet on their estates, they were obviously biding their time
for revenge. Mehemet Aly looked forward : if he could snatch
a victory out of the trap the Sultan had laid : if he could, at
the same time, rid himself of this anomalous, mediæval encum-
brance of the Mameluke emirs, then he would at last, really
be master of his kingdom, and, in time maybe, of very much
more.

There was no time to lose and he started off at once to make
friendly overtures to the emirs and to allay their suspicions
of him, then, when preparations were completed for sending
off the expedition to Arabia under his son Toussoun, he
issued invitations for a ceremony to be held at the Citadel.
Toussoun was to be presented with a pelisse of honour and

subsequently escorted, with his army, to the gates of Cairo.
Nearly all the Mamelukes fell into the trap. Five hundred
of them, attired and caparisoned with all their accustomed
magnificence, gathered in Nasr's great Diwan, where they
were received in state by Mehemet Aly and entertained to
refreshments. After the banquet and the presentations,
the procession formed up in the courtyard, a splendid body
of men, superbly mounted and followed by a gorgeous retinue.
The Turkish Janissaries led the way, followed by the Pasha's
Albanian bodyguard ; then the Mamelukes, all on horseback,
with some Turkish regulars at the rear, filed away down the
steep and narrow road to the Bab el Azab. When the Janissaries had passed out into the Place Rumeyla, a signal was
given, the gate was closed, the Albanians turned upon the
Mamelukes and the massacre began. The emirs had not the
shadow of a chance, for not only were they caught in the
narrow roadway entirely unprepared, but the Turkish soldiers
from behind and from above fired upon any who sought safety
in a return to the Palace, and not one of the unhappy Beys,
who had ridden up that morning in such pomp and pride, was
left alive when the evening fell. The tale of the one Mameluke who escaped by urging his horse over the cliff, seems to
be a picturesque fiction, the facts being that Amin Bey, the
survivor, of whom it is told, was late in arriving, saw the
head of the procession emerging from the Bab el Azab and
the closing of the gate. That was enough ; he compre-
hended in a flash the Pasha's treachery, set spurs to his horse
and fled away to Syria.

Some few others, who had distrusted the invitation and
not attended the ceremony, also managed to get out of Egypt
and took refuge in the Sudan, but that terrible day, which
drenched the Citadel in blood, was the end of the Mameluke
emirs, as it was the end of the mediæval fortress.

CHAPTER VII

CAIRO: THE MONUMENTS

THOUGH much has been written and much has been said about Arab art, no art or architecture ever came out of the sandy wastes of Arabia. Ideas came, and fervid enthusiasm, but the desert nomads never had a civilization or a culture of their own. Yet, where their religion arose there must needs have been places of worship where the austere and rigid ritual had its origin. Assuredly the first place where Mohammed's followers assembled to pray was at Mohammed's house. It was a courtyard in Medina, surrounded by a brick wall, with a couple of doors at the side which opened into the huts of Mohammed's wives. As shelter from the burning sun, some palm trunks were set up at one end and roofed over with palm branches. Nothing more simple or more primitive could be imagined, but in that open court, with its rough shelter under the palm boughs, we can see, clearly enough, the beginnings of the mosque. When the prophet died and his warlike Arabs spread out on their career of conquest to the north and east and west, they came up against three advanced civilizations, in Mesopotamia, Syria and Egypt. In all three were splendid buildings, such as they had never seen or dreamt of in their desert home. In Mesopotamia the building was Persian, with some influence still of ancient Babylonia; in Syria it was mostly Byzantine, in Egypt also Byzantine, but with some different features. In all these places it was the inhabitants of the countries who, under the Moslem conquerors, carried out the architecture that was required for the new worship. It developed in a different way in all three, but the dominant forces in Moham-

medan building came from the first two.   The rulers of Egypt
were never Egyptians ; they brought their ideas and often
their architects from Damascus or the Euphrates.   It is in
the lesser arts that the skill of the Coptic craftsmen makes
itself felt, such as the glasswork and the fine inlaid screens
of wood and ivory, which are indistinguishable in style in the
mosques and in the ancient churches.   Perhaps the chief
contribution made by Egypt to the mosque architecture is
the pulpit, which is known in a Coptic Monastery of the sixth
century.   It became the " mimbar " of the mosque, from
which the Koran was preached, but it was not present in
the early mosques.

In the chapter on the Coptic churches, we have seen what
the richness of Egypt was when the Arabs came and the
contrast of the simple little mosque of Amr at Fustat, compared with the Christian churches.   Amr's mosque was
practically the same as the house of Mohammed ; an open
courtyard, with his house adjoining.   That was built only
nine years after the death of the prophet, and two centuries
went by without any sign of progress or advance on this
elementary beginning.   There is no record of any good building at all, until, suddenly, there comes the mosque of Ibn
Tulun, which is one of the finest in the world.   It seems
very surprising, but, as we have indicated, the reason lies
outside of Egypt, and development was going on rapidly
elsewhere.   For a short time the capital of Islam was at
Damascus, but was transferred to Baghdad, where, under the
Abbasid caliphs, who were not pure Arabs, a tremendous
expansion began.

At Samarra, on the Tigris, there still stands a very early
mosque, which marks an important stage in the evolution
of Moslem architecture.   It consists of a great, oblong, arcaded
courtyard ; at the end of it, instead of the old, rude shelter
of palm logs and branches, is a colonnade of brick, the columns
and arches elaborately decorated with stucco ornament.   And
an important new feature has been added.   In the centre of
the northern end, but outside the mosque, is a strangely
shaped tower, like a tall, blunt cone, with an outside stair

winding up it. This is an obvious descendant of the old
Babylonian " ziggurat," but it is likewise one of the ancestors
of the minaret.

The centre of power was in Mesopotamia, and Egypt was
of no account politically ; it was merely a province of the
caliphate and bled white for tribute ; much of the population
was Christian, but the fine old churches of Babylon were
hiding more and more from dangerous notice ; Cairo did
not yet exist and Fustat was little more than a collection of
mud houses trying to be inconspicuous enough to escape the
notice of the tax-gatherers. At length, however, in A.D. 868,
a man came to Egypt as governor, who was strong enough
to make her practically independent of Baghdad and able
to spend her income on herself. This was Ahmed Ibn Tulun,
a Turk by race and a man of Samarra, who came from the
court of the Caliph and had all the training and education that
Baghdad could give. When he had raised himself to supreme
power in Egypt, he required something better to house his
kingly retinue and to carry on his stately worship than Fustat
could offer, so he moved the town nearer to the Mokattam
hills and built his mosque, with his palace adjoining it, not
far from the foot of the cliff where the Citadel afterwards
rose (Plate VI).

His palace is said to have been magnificent, but it has
totally disappeared. The mosque remains, and lo ! it is
the mosque of Samarra over again ! The brick building, the
rows of columns, the plaster ornament, are so much alike
that it cannot fail to strike anyone who sees plans or photographs of them. The minaret, too, which stands, not as the
minarets of later mosques, at the corners, but alone, in the
centre of the north-west wall, is without doubt derived from
Samarra. This minaret has been the subject of much discussion : it has been instanced to prove that the minaret
was evolved from the Pharos of Alexandria ; but it has been
likewise instanced to prove that the minaret had nothing to
do with the Pharos and could only have come from the
Samarra tower ! There seemed to be a great deal to say on
both sides, but the whole question is linked up with yet

PLATE VI

MINARET OF MOSQUE OF IBN TÛLÛN

another factor, in the development of which more hereafter. As to the minaret of Ibn Tulun, Captain Creswell informs me that it is without doubt a restoration of the thirteenth century, but that the top part of the cone—not the top of the minaret —retains the corkscrew form of the Samarra tower, of which the original minaret was almost certainly a copy.

The dynasty of Ibn Tulun was short-lived and was followed by an unsettled period, which came to an end with the Fatimite invasion from the West. This brought about a religious as well as a political change. The Fatimites took their name from Fatima, the daughter of Mohammed, in whose line, they maintained, the succession ought to have remained. Fatima had married Aly, who was appointed the fourth caliph, but he was murdered and his children dispossessed. There had always been adherents, however, who believed that the descendants of the prophet, through Fatima, were the rightful heads of the religion. About the beginning of the tenth century, a vigorous propaganda was carried on throughout the Muslim world, which had important results; chiefly notable, for us, by the conquests of Tunis and the establishment there of a Fatimite caliph. From Kairouan these Shi'ite conquerors spread rapidly over North Africa and Sicily. The fourth caliph of the line, El Muezz, seeing the wealth and weakness of Egypt, made an expedition against it and subdued the country without much difficulty. It was noted in the chapter on the Citadel, how Gohar or Gawhar, his victorious general, founded the town of Cairo. This inaugurated a new era of building and a great expansion of power. Four or five mosques, three great gates and a considerable stretch of the walls built by the Fatimites still remain, but a change came in the type of architecture from the Mesopotamian traditions which we saw in the mosque of Ibn Tulun. The Fatimites, although they came into Egypt from the West, were recent invaders there and were more influenced by the art and customs of North Syria, which they had quitted only a few generations before. The Fatimite buildings are of stone, square and rather fortress-like, but the earlier mosques were similar to Ibn Tulun's in plan, and decorated, like his, with stucco ornament. They have a large open court, arcaded all round, with several rows of columns at the south-eastern end, above the sanctuary. In the centre of the south-eastern wall is the " mihrab " or " Kibleh," the prayer niche, always placed so that the worshippers face Mecca when performing their devotions. A curious point is that, although this is the holy place and the orientation of the whole building had to conform to it, the universal custom was that a mosque opened directly from the street. Now, a street may run in any direction, and every street in mediæval Cairo winds and curves about, so the entrances to the mosques vary in plan according to the amount of contrivance required by the architects to get the congregation into the sacred enclosure.

The most ancient of the Fatimite mosques is El Azhar, the University, which numbers ten or twelve thousand students and has overflowed, for the teaching of the junior classes, into El Moayyed and others.

Naturally, many sultans have made additions and alterations to a place of such importance, but the most drastic were not carried out until the eighteenth century, under a Turkish emir called Abderrahman. He enlarged the mosque considerably and, in order to do this, took away the entire south-eastern wall, except the " mihrab " and built a large addition behind it, so that now, when we first enter, the place looks like a forest of pillars, with a rather meaningless niche and bit of wall standing in the middle. The Turkish work is much inferior to the old building, but, at first sight, especially if the floor is covered by groups of students listening to the sheikh who teaches, or themselves reciting the lesson in the orthodox sing-song voice, the effect is so bewildering that one can hardly grasp the niceties of architecture.

Round the open court of El Azhar are rooms for foreign students, for the University is frequented by all the Muslim world and we may note the complexions of Turkey, Morocco and the Sudan among the students, many of whom live as well as study within its walls. When the classes break off for the midday interval, the floor is quickly dotted over with little companies, who settle down to their lunch of bread and vegetables, while the water-carrier goes the rounds, supplying drink for the thirsty from his bulging water-skin.

The course takes twelve years and the instruction is almost entirely confined to Muslim law, as expounded in the Koran and its commentators, but I understand that of late years some slight concessions have been made to more modern views of education.

The next mosque in date to El Azhar is that of El Hakem, who succeeded in A.D. 996 as a boy of eleven and lasted till A.D. 1021. The story of his rule is a kind of historical nightmare, for he was at the same time a religious fanatic and a monster of cruelty. The most blood-curdling tales are told of the ferocity of the tortures that he inflicted and the most grotesque ones of his outbursts of reforming zeal. All amusements were forbidden and the life of the town was changed from day to night, for he had a passion for the dark and even marketing could only be begun after sunset. Women might not leave their houses and he went so far as to forbid all the shoemakers to make shoes for them, lest they should be tempted out of doors on any pretext. As his madness grew on him, he took to wandering farther and farther away by night, alone, and at length met his end out on the Mokattam hills. He believed that he was divine and immune to every attack, and the most extraordinary thing about the story is that he found some people who accepted his claims.

One of these, a Persian called Durazi, nearly stirred up a revolution by ordering the preacher in the mosque of Amr to begin, instead of with the usual invocation to God, by the words " In the Name of El Hakem, the Compassionate, the Merciful." The blaspheming sheikh was put to death by the outraged congregation and Durazi was pursued through Cairo, but he reached the Palace and was protected by El Hakem, who stoutly denied his presence there, and finally got him off to Syria, where he founded the sect of the Druses, who to this day believe that El Hakem will one day reappear as the Incarnation of the Divine Wisdom. His death gave them renewed assurance that he was more than mortal ; the

7

body was never found, only his coat, pierced through by dagger thrusts, was brought back to Cairo.

The mosque was much damaged by an earthquake which occurred in A.D. 1303, and the reconstruction of it, soon after that date, has given rise to many architectural problems, too technical to be entered on here. The mosque adjoins the Walls of Cairo, but was built about fifty years earlier. All visitors to the Walls, and that ought to be every one who has the chance to go, should enter through the mosque of El Hakem and ascend to the Bab el Futuh by a stair inside the outer shell of the minaret, which gives a most interesting view of the beautiful and ancient decoration of the circular tower within. It is the original minaret, and is adorned with some of the best and most characteristic Fatimite ornament. The outer masonry was built up round it to brace it after the earthquake.

To my thinking, the walls are the most impressive of all the Fatimite monuments. Their date is easy to remember, as they were completed about 1087, a few years after the Norman conquest of England. Evil days had fallen on Egypt, famine and plague, and fighting between the Turkish and Nubian soldiers who garrisoned the country. The caliph Mustansir, El Hakem's grandson, who reigned for about sixty years, was compelled to apply for help to an Armenian general, Bedr el Gamaly, who had been a slave, but had risen to high military rank and been appointed governor of Acre. Bedr el Gamaly agreed to come, on condition that he should bring his Syrian troops with him, and he got Egypt into order with ruthless severity, but ruled it afterwards, on behalf of the caliph, with justice and benevolence. Egypt is always wealthy when it is well governed and Bedr el Gamaly employed part of the increased revenues in building fortifications suitable to the capital. He brought three Armenian brothers from Edessa, as architects to superintend the work, and the three gates which remain are severally attributed to them. These are the Bab el Futuh and the Bab el Nasr, to the north of the town, close to El Hakem's mosque ; and the Bab el Zuweila, at the opposite end of the Fatimite city. Between the two first named is a long stretch of wall which can be visited and thoroughly explored. All the way along are large internal galleries, with guard rooms at intervals. On the outer side are arrow slits for the defenders and above the gates are openings through which molten lead or other fiery armour could be poured down on the roadway below. Above are towers and battlements; the whole affording shelter for an enormous garrison. The masonry is particularly fine; the Armenian builders set a new standard for that. I do not know anything finer of its kind than the vaulting of the stairways down to the gates. We cannot help noticing as we pass that many blocks of ancient Egyptian sculpture, torn from the tombs of Giza, were built into these Saracenic walls; they are used any side up, just because they were good bits of stone, and most probably there are many others with the faces turned inwards and so escaping detection. Another curious detail is that every tower bears a French name; Napoleon, when he occupied Cairo, put troops upon the walls and did a certain amount of repair on some of the forts.

The streets leading from the Bab el Futuh and the Bab el Nasr converge and meet a short distance within the town and form what used to be the main artery of Cairo, running straight through to the Bab el Zuweila. A most interesting street it is, though its character is changing very rapidly. The Bab el Zuweila, now in the midst of a busy quarter, has become a kind of popular sanctuary, owing to its once having been the residence of a holy man, and it is more often called after him, the Bab el Mitwally, than by its proper name. The nails which stud the gate are always hung with rags or bits of hair; offerings to the sheikh from sick people, for his healing efficacy is supposed to persist, if something belonging to the patient is left in the vicinity.

On each of the towers there stands a fine minaret, belonging to the neighbouring mosque of El Moayyed, of a much later date than the gateway.

The Fatimites ended with the coming of Saladin and a new era of building began. We have seen, on the Citadel hill, how his fortifications still surround the northern enclosure, and part of the City walls also remain. These were intended to enclose a much larger area than the old Fatimite walls had done. At that time the Nile flowed where now is the station square, and Saladin's walls began there and traversed the present northern quarters of Cairo, turning southwards at the Burg el Zafar, where a considerable portion of them is still to be seen, but his scheme of continuing the circuit round to include the mosque of Ibn Tulun and part, at least, of Fustat, was never carried out.

Saladin's religious innovations were very important. He was the champion of orthodox Islam, who had recovered Egypt from the Shi'ite Fatimites and he was resolved to educate his people in the right paths. He founded colleges both in Alexandria and Cairo, none of which survive, but the effect upon the architecture of mosques was immediate and remarkable. After his time most of the mosques are "medresas"—colleges—as well as houses of prayer.

It used to be said that Saladin initiated the cruciform mosque, which is the type much best known to most people. It consists of a central court, covered or open, with four deep porticoes, or "liwans," slightly raised, in which the sheikhs of the four orthodox sects of Islam gave instruction to their disciples. Within the last few years, however, Captain Creswell's researches have brought out the fact that the first of the Ayubite mosques were on a much simpler plan and that the cruciform type did not appear until a century later. The early Medresa-mosque seems to have been evolved out of the architecture of private houses.

Most of the mediæval houses had a large and spacious hall, much longer than it was broad, with a fountain in the middle, and the ends raised, by one or two steps, above the centre.

Under Saladin and his Ayubite successors, the medresas were built very much in this manner ; the central part, where the fountain was, being enlarged into a kind of courtyard, and the two ends becoming the "liwans" where the students gathered for study.

Unfortunately all the mosques of this period have been so much altered that one cannot point to any typical example. The mausoleum of Imam el Shafey, in the district known as the " Tombs of the Mamelukes," was built by the wife of El Adil Saphedin, and contains a good deal of fine contemporary work. It is an interesting place, but not an easy one to see, as it has a great reputation for sanctity, and visitors are not welcomed, unless accompanied by some one who has acquaintances there. The mosque is quite modern, but it also has an interest, for nowhere else have I seen a mosque so much frequented by all classes at all hours of the day. Perhaps, along with Saida Zeinab, whose mosque is much resorted to by women, Imam el Shafey may be said to be the most popular saint of Cairo.

After the Ayubites came the Turkish, or Baharite Mamelukes, the first of whom were Shegeret el Dur and her second husband, Aybek, but the real founder was Beybars. He brought Egypt to great glory and prosperity by his defeat of the Mongols, who had overrun the East, captured Baghdad and pushed down through Palestine as far as Gaza. Beybars met them there, drove back the garrison and finally inflicted a crushing blow on the undisciplined hordes of Tartars near Beisan, east of the plain of Megiddo.

Beybars, or, to give him his entire name, the Sultan el Melik el Daher Rukn el Dunya wa el Din, Beybars el Bundukdari el Salihi, built a huge mosque, now known as " Daher." It stands outside the circuit of the old walls, on the way to Abbassieh : though much ruined it presents interesting features and preserves a certain amount of the original ornament, which is bold and fine, like the Fatimite. In it there seems to have been the first example in Egypt of a large dome, which was probably borrowed from Syria.

The problem of how to build a dome upon a square base had been solved long before this time, by the Byzantine architects. The great triumph was St. Sophia in Constantinople, but there are plenty of examples of it in Europe as well as farther east. It is pre-Islamic, but this style of building was little used in Egypt in the early Moslem buildings, though

in the time of the Mameluke Sultans, it became the chief
feature of the architecture.

After Beybars the number of splendid mosques and mauso-
leums is amazing. Owing to the devastation of Mesopotamia
and Syria by the Mongols, Egypt was crowded with refugees
from these countries, who brought with them all the skill
in crafts and industries that had flourished there among the
Christian and Muslim inhabitants, so that for the next three
centuries, Cairo was the centre of Islam and Islamic culture.

A wonderful group of buildings stands in the " Nahassin,"
or copper bazaar a little way beyond the entrance to the
well-known " Khan el Khalil." The most remarkable of
these is the Mausoleum of the Sultan Kalaun, which is architecturally unique. The lofty dome rests, not on the walls,
but on piers and columns, with a sort of ambulatory surrounding them. The effect is magnificent ; it is undoubtedly one
of the most impressive buildings in Cairo. His mosque is
close by and also a " Muristan," or hospital, which he founded,
it is said, in fulfilment of a vow, made once when he lay sick
in Damascus. This was the first hospital in Egypt, and
was provided with every medical appliance known to the age.
Next door to Kalaun's Mausoleum is the college-mosque of
his son, Nasr Mohammed ibn el Kalaun, a very great man,
much of whose work has been noted in our chapter on the
Citadel. This mosque has a Gothic doorway, which was
brought from a Crusaders' church at Acre and set up here, in
the midst of the imposing buildings of Islam. Several other
bits of Crusaders' workmanship are to be seen, which must
have been moved to Cairo about this time, columns and
pilasters carved with figures and scenes, in strange sharp
contrast to the geometric designs prescribed by Moham-
medanism.

Acknowledged supreme, in beauty and splendour, is the
college mosque of Sultan Hassan, one of Nasr's sons, notable
for no other achievement, but ever to be remembered for his
noble building. The exterior is fine, with its lofty portal
and the heavy frieze, which crowns its bare and massive walls,
but it is the interior aspect that makes the deepest impression.

It is the typical cruciform mosque, with four liwans, the largest, where prayers are said, superbly decorated with a broad bold frieze of Kufic characters and a rich pulpit and " mihrab." It surely must be one of the greatest Muslim buildings in the world, for all the qualities of Mohammedan architecture are there at their best ; the majestic simplicity of the open court, the noble proportions of the liwans, the ornament, so sparingly used, yet, when it is used, so rich in its effect, all combine to arouse in us the feeling of solemnity and awe that is inspired by the sight of a great cathedral.

It would be out of place to enter upon a detailed description of the beautiful mosques that can be visited, but those who desire to see them intelligently are referred to Mrs. Devonshire's " Rambles and Studies in Cairo." Perhaps it may be of interest to some readers if I say a little at this point about the development of the minaret, which has been the subject of much controversy.

Attractive as the idea is that the minaret was derived from the other great light-tower, the Pharos of Alexandria, it does not seem to stand a close examination.

After careful researches in Syria as well as in Egypt, Captain Creswell has arrived at the following conclusions. We have seen that the minaret of Ibn Tulun's mosque, though a later reconstruction and not a contemporary building, carries strong evidence that the original minaret was a direct descendant of the one at Samarra in Mesopotamia. The two next, at the mosque of El Hakem, are circular, and though quite different in style from that of Ibn Tulun, are very definitely of Mesopotamian design. But there the development in this direction is arrested : there are no other examples ; and under the Mameluke sultans, another type began which takes its origin from the Syrian church towers, which were square, and topped by a little pointed dome resting on pillars. The conquest of Syria had followed a different line from that of Egypt and the victorious Muslims had taken possession of the churches there and used them as mosques, with little alteration, so that in course of time, all idea of Christian origin must have been entirely lost. The early minarets of this second style in Cairo are all square, but the decoration of the pillars round the top gradually becomes elongated and much more elaborate. The dome and pillars, in fact, squeezed down the square tower, until, in the final stage, the tower only reached to the height of the mosque roof, from which the minaret rises in a series of octagons, richly decorated and always terminated by the little dome at the top.

Many examples of this process of evolution are to be seen in Cairo. The minarets of El Moayyed's mosque, which are built upon the towers of the old Bab el Zuweila, are fine specimens of a rather late stage. The minarets built after the Turkish conquest are of still another type; very slender, round, and much less decorated.

Another mosque which ought to be mentioned is that of Aqsankur, who was a vizier of Nasr ibn el Kalaun's. It is, for some reason, a great favourite with tourists and one to which dragomans almost invariably take their parties. Its main attraction is not the original building, but the restoration which took place in the Turkish period, under Ibrahim Aga, when the wall of the sanctuary was covered with tiles, from which it has acquired the name of the " Blue mosque." It is a very pretty little place, worth seeing, but has no architectural features of much interest.

During the period of the Circassian Mamelukes, perhaps the most remarkable development is the beautiful dome building in stone, with outside ornament (Plate V. 2. gives a particularly fine example).

The mosques were as rich and elaborate as ever—more so, indeed, and for that very reason they lose something in impressiveness.

In the Arab Museum, where the smaller objects from mosques and houses are collected, this is very marked. The older pieces, the few Fatimite wood carvings, for instance, are fine and strong in design, but the intricacy of pattern on all the later work, whether in wood or metal, becomes fatiguing to the eye. The same must be said of the illuminated manuscripts in the Royal Library, which are superb of their kind, but monotonous. An art bound down to such narrow limits.

forbidden to seek inspiration from living form, could not possibly avoid falling into this snare of over-ornateness and unreality. Exception must be made of the lamps, which are among the most lovely things ever made of glass. They were certainly made by Egyptian workmen, who adapted the ornament prescribed by Islam to their own ancient Coptic forms.

Out on the north side of Cairo is a curious cemetery; generally, though quite erroneously, known as the " Tombs of the Caliphs." It was only during the rule of the unorthodox Fatimites, who did not acknowledge the Caliph of Baghdad as the successor of the Prophet, that the rulers of Egypt took the title of Caliph ; the Sultans from Saladin onwards never professed themselves to be the religious heads of Islam. Still, for convenience, one always does talk of the Tombs of the Caliphs when one means the Tombs of the Circassian Mamelukes. The place is so extraordinarily picturesque that it is well worth going to see, if only to drive through it, but the Mausoleum of Barkuk (Plate V. 2.), the first of these Sultans, is interesting and very beautiful, not so much for any one feature as for its whole character. Personally, I like it much better than the neighbouring one of Kait Bey, which is in better repair and is much more often visited, but suffers, like so many of the later buildings, from over-ornateness.

With the coming of the Turks, Egypt's glory passed away and the later buildings of Cairo show a sad falling off. One or two Turkish mosques are worth seeing, especially that of Mohammed Abu Dahab, near El Azhar, and the very small, but rich and charming one of Bordeini, in a lane not far from the Sharia Mehemet Aly.

When we come to modern times, we have Mehemet Aly's large mosque in the Citadel, about which something must be said, for it is generally the one which tourists are taken first to see. That, in itself, is a misfortune. The gaudy interior, the alabaster courtyard, the big white building, are all so showy that they give a wrong idea of what a mosque ought to be ; they vitiate the taste, as it were, before it has had time to get formed ; and, when the new-comers go down the hill and see the sublime severity of Sultan Hassan's great liwans with the arch of heaven above his centre court, many of them feel that it is cold and bare.

But in spite of all its faults, the mosque of Mehemet Aly is such a feature in the landscape, its tall minarets stand out so clear in every view of Cairo, that one has learned to accept it as being part of the natural order of things.   So deeply has the old Albanian left his mark upon Egypt !

CHAPTER VIII

CAIRO: THE MEDIÆVAL TOWN

IN every book of travel written after the middle of last century, there is complaint of the change and loss of picturesqueness of Cairo. I suppose that the people who were there before that were too much occupied in living in it to notice, and that, by the time it began to be looked upon as a show place, the modernizing had already gone a certain distance. Yet it seems to me that, even now, the streets and lanes are full of entertainment and that pictures offer themselves at every turn. But it is not possible, nowadays, to see it without some effort.

When I knew Cairo first, in the 'nineties of last century, it was much easier. The old way of everybody going about on donkeys was passing away and cabs and bicycles were coming in, but the traffic was slow, and one could walk about and take time to look at things, even in the Mousky and the wider streets. Now, motors hoot along the narrow roadways and the noise, dust and danger to life increase with every month that passes.

Most people go to the bazaars in Khan el Khalil, which are animated and picturesque, but entirely laid out for the seduction of tourists; after that, one or two mosques are visited and then the old parts are given up and people drive out to see the races or to watch the polo at Gezira and sigh over the deterioration of Cairo; "Quite a European town now, so disappointing." It is quite true that the European part of Cairo *is* a European town, but that is what has saved, for a time at least, the Arab quarters.

We may still get some idea of the old life of the place, if

we have time and energy, and, if possible, a little Arabic. And we must walk.

If we turn out of the Mousky to the right and go into the bazaars behind the mosque of El Ghury, we find a whole line of covered lanes where scents, dyes and spices are sold and manufactured, silks are woven, carpets and scarves that come in from Tunis are laid out in the booths and the general appearance of the place is very Oriental. Indeed almost anywhere, if we leave the main thoroughfares and go into the lanes that surround them, we shall find a great deal to look at, but to understand what the aspect of Cairo was a hundred years or more ago, we must help ourselves out by reading what old travellers say.

Until the middle of last century nothing of the present European quarter existed. Between the Ezbekieh and the Nile was a stretch of open country, traversed by the road to Boulac, the port of Cairo, then a separate little town on the river bank. The Mousky, which was the first street, in the western sense, that pierced through the network of winding lanes that formed the mediæval city, was begun under Napoleon and carried through at different times after him. What is now the Ezbekieh garden was an open field, which in the time of high Nile became a lake. There were two or three other such sheets of water in the middle of the town and the old canal, which connected the Nile with the Red Sea, meandered through it, but was only navigable in flood time, so the appearance of the place varied very much according to the season of the year. There were good houses and gardens along the line of the canal, but the finest were round the Ezbekieh, where most of the wealthy Mameluke emirs had their palaces.

There are countless descriptions of Cairo in old books of travel, some of which are excellent and surprise us by the justness of observation and by the amount the writers contrived to see, but, as a rule, they do not find much that pleases them about the buildings. The beauty of Mohammedan architecture does not seem to have appealed to the eighteenth-century European. The narrowness of the streets shocked

them and the massive, plain exterior of the typical Turkish
houses appeared gloomy and repellent. On the other hand
they were, one and all, much struck with the sheets of water
about the town, varying with the changing year from lakes to
verdant meadows.

The following extract is from Pococke's travels. He was
an English clergyman who visited Egypt in 1737, well back
in the period of Turkish rule.

" If one imagines that there are several squares or places
about the city, from a quarter to three-quarters of a mile
round, contrived so as to receive and hold the water of the
Nile, that is conveyed to them by the canals when the river
rises, it may give some idea of the several lakes that are about
the city during the greater part of the year ; and nothing can
be imagined more beautiful than to see those places fill'd
with water, round which the best houses in the city are built ;
and when the Nile is high in the summer, it must be an entertaining prospect to see them covered with the fine boats and
barges of all the great people, who come out in the evening
to divert themselves with their ladies. As I have been in-
formed, concerts of music are never wanting, and sometimes
fireworks add to the amusement, all the houses round being
in a manner illuminated, and the windows full of spectators
to behold this glorious sight. The scene is much altered
when the waters are gone off, and nothing but mud appears ;
but is soon succeeded by a more agreeable view of green corn,
and afterwards of harvest, in the middle of a great city, on
those very spots where the boats were sailing a few months
before.

" The streets of Cairo, as of all the Turkish cities, are very
narrow : the widest goes the length of the city from the gate
Nasser to the gate Zuile, but would be looked on as a lane in
Europe. The other streets are so narrow, that they frequently
make a roof from one house to the other over the street, and
put a slight covering on it to defend them from the sun. The
city of Cairo is exceedingly well regulated for its security,
more especially by night ; for most of the streets, or at least
each end of every district or ward, has a gate and porter to it,
who shuts up the gate as soon as it is dark, and to every one of
these wards is a guard of two or three or more janizaries, so

that no idle people can go about the streets at night. Some little streets consist only of shops, without any houses, and so they leave their shops locked up, and go to their houses at night. There are also several places for shops like our exchanges, called Bezestans, which are shut up at night, and shops of the same trade are generally together in these as well as in the streets.

" Turkish houses, especially in Cairo, have very little beauty in them ; they are generally built round a court, where they make the best appearance, nothing but use being considered as to the outside of their houses, what they have of ornament being in their saloons within ; so that their houses, built below of stone and above a sort of cage work, sometimes filled up with unburnt brick, and few or no windows towards the street, are a very disagreeable sight to one who has seen only European cities, that have something of outward regularity, as well as conveniency and beauty within."

Pococke goes on later in the book :

" They have also several canes (*Khans*—caravanserais) in Cairo, which they call here Okelas, they are very indifferent buildings round a court, are commonly appropriated to merchants of a particular, with their merchandise ; as there is one for those of Nubia, and the black slaves and other goods they bring along with them ; another for white slaves from Georgia ; they have also several canes at Bulac, in all which strangers are accommodated with a room at a very small price, but with nothing else ; so that excepting the room, there are no greater accommodations in these houses than there are in the deserts, unless from the conveniency of a market near.

" I went to see some of the best houses in Cairo. The great men have a saloon for common use, and another for state, and as they have four wives, each of them has a saloon, with the apartments about it, that have no communication with the other parts of the house, except the common entrance for the servants, which is kept lock'd ; and the private entrance, of which the master keeps the key. They have such a machine made to turn round, as they use in nunneries, which receives any thing they want to give in or out, without seeing one another. At the house of Osman Bey, there is a fine saloon

with a lobby before it ; the grand room is an oblong square ;
in the middle is an octagon marble pillar ; the room is wains-
cotted on two sides about eight feet high, in pannels of grey
marble, with a border round every pannel of mosaic work ;
the end at which one enters, and the side where the windows
are, not being finish'd in this manner ; the sopha extends all
round the room, and the whole is furnish'd with the richest
velvet cushions, and the floor cover'd with fine carpets."

Pococke's account of the life of European residents is
pleasant.

" The European merchants here, considering how much
they are confined, live agreeably enough among themselves,
are generally sociable with those of their own nation, and in a
plentiful country they do not want whatever may make life
pass agreeably. The morning being spent in business, the
remainder of the day is often passed in riding out to the fields
and gardens to the north of Cairo, where for a mile out of town
there is little danger ; sometimes the whole day is spent in
diversion that way, and they have a relaxation from business
both on the Christian and Jewish Sabbath, as the Jews trans-
act a great part of their affairs. When the Nile is high and
little business is done, they spend their time in the houses
they have at Old Cairo and Gize, so that strangers pass their
time as agreeably as the circumstances of the place will permit, the gentlemen here showing them all manner of civility,
especially such as come out of curiosity, who never fail to
meet with a kind reception in their houses, which they easily
oblige them to make their home, as it is very difficult to be
otherwise accommodated here."

A later picture of Cairo, and a very lively one, is from Denon,
who was one of the scientific members of Napoleon's expedition. He arrived in Cairo just in time to hear that a party
was going to the Pyramids and seized upon the chance to
accompany it. This was almost immediately after the Battle
of the Pyramids and the country was in an extremely dangerous state, so the only way to go was under the protection
of a strong military escort.
He says :

" We arrived at Gizeh after nightfall : I had no idea where
I should sleep, but having been fully prepared for a simple
bivouac, it seemed to me a stroke of good fortune verging on
the miraculous to find myself reposing on velvet-covered
divans, in a hall where the scent of orange blossom was wafted
in on refreshing breezes from shady bowers. This house was
the country retreat—' maison de plaisance ' of Murad Bey "
(one of the Mameluke leaders). " I had heard it spoken of
depreciatingly, I only saw it after the passage of a conquering
army, yet, I could not help feeling that, if one will only abstain
from profitless comparisons, a good deal of merit is to be found
in the Oriental notion of pleasure and the abandonment of
one's senses to the voluptuous ease in which it envelopes us.
" We find here neither the long and stately avenues of
France nor the winding paths of English gardens ; these gardens which invite to active exercise and bring us health and
hunger as its reward. In the East, all unnecessary exertion
is banished from the category of enjoyments. From the cool
shade thrown by the bending boughs of a clump of sycamores,
we enter tents or kiosques which open at will on sweet scented
groves of oranges or jasmine : add to this, delights which as
yet we have hardly experienced, but can picture all their
charm, as, for instance, the joy of being waited on by young
slave girls, graceful in form, sweet and caressing in manner."

Delightful as Murad's garden seems to have been, Denon
did leave it and go on to the Pyramids, and when he and
his friends actually got the chance to see some of the fascinating *jeunes esclaves* in the flesh, they were more than a little
disillusioned.
The following passage is from the Appendix to Denon's
book, and is by another writer, Norry by name.

" At length we had the opportunity to behold, not indeed
in Turkish houses, but in the quarters of some of our General
officers, some of the slave women who had been found in the
hareems after the flight of the Beys and taken under the care
of these generals. These beauties have been much over-
praised : they are almost all excessively fat and have neither
elegance, grace, nor freedom of movement.
" The caravans from Abyssinia having just arrived, bringing

young black girls to be sold in the bazars where this barbarous commerce is carried on, we went to see these unhappy creatures. They were packed by ten or twelve into little rooms, where, lying naked on the floor, they were grinding a few grains of corn between stones to make their bread."

He goes on to say that "le Général Bonaparte" absolutely forbade any of his officers to buy slaves, but of course, had no opportunity to do anything else to discourage the traffic.

Returning to Denon's description, I quote part of his impressions of Cairo and Cairo life. He did not see much picturesqueness about it, but his account is graphic and amusing.

"After nearly a month in Cairo, I still sought in vain for this superb town, this holy city, great among the great, the delight of the soul, as Oriental writers call it. What I actually saw was an immense population, vast distances to traverse, but never a fine street, never a monument. One place indeed, Lelbequier (El Ezbekieh) where General Bonaparte lived, is enormous, but looks like a field. This, at the time of the inundation, has a certain charm, owing to its coolness and the pleasantness of boating on it by night.

"The palaces of the rich, surrounded by high walls, make the streets more sombre than beautiful, while the dwellings of the poor look more miserable here than elsewhere, since to all the evils of poverty are added the negligence and disorderliness induced by the climate.

"However, once one has penetrated into these gloomy fortresses, one does find some measure of comfort, some endeavour after beauty and well-being : marble baths, luxuriously heated ; halls decorated with mosaic with basins and fountains in the centre ; large divans or wide benches thickly upholstered, covered with rugs and costly fabrics and strewn with splendid cushions. These divans generally go round three sides of the room. The windows, when there are any, are never opened and the light from them falls dimly through tiny panes of coloured glass, set deeply in a grid-like frame. The room is principally lighted from a dome in the middle of the roof. The Muslims, unacquainted with all the uses we make of light, give themselves little trouble to procure it : in truth, all their customs seem to conduce to repose. Their

8

divans, on which one lies rather than sits, are so comfortable that it is an effort to get up : their clothes, with long skirts enveloping their legs, big sleeves that fall eight inches beyond the finger tips, and a turban which prevents them from moving their heads : their habit of holding in one hand a pipe which intoxicates them with its heavy odours, in the other a chaplet of beads, which they pass through their fingers, all contribute to the utter destruction of activity and imagination.

" Such beings as are obliged to do any work are not very different. They have accustomed their employers to expect nothing from their labour that in any manner departs from the ordinary routine, which they never forsake. They never invent a way of doing better, and, especially do they reject every device which would compel them to stand upright, a thing they detest above all others. Carpenters, locksmiths, joiners, blacksmiths, all work seated ; a mason will even build a minaret without ever standing up."

I think, when Denon wrote that, he must have been trying to get some work done, and come across a silent opposition that he did not quite understand. But there is enough truth in the picture to make it worth quoting.

The next glimpse of Cairo is from Belzoni, who was there early in the reign of Mehemet Aly, from 1815 onwards. He did not go as a tourist, nor with a conquering army ; but as an engineer, who had invented a machine for raising water, which he hoped to get accepted by the Pasha.

He stayed a long time in Egypt and wrote an exceedingly interesting book about his experiences there, from which I shall have occasion to quote in later chapters. As he was a poor man with none of the protection or advantages that a wealthy traveller could command, one feels that his testimony has, or ought to have, considerable value. He and his wife rented a tumble-down house at Boulac, where they stayed until the Pasha gave them quarters at Shubra, in order to try the invention in his garden. According to Belzoni, the machine was a complete success, but the Pasha was so much worked on by intriguers that he finally declined to take it. Meantime, however, Belzoni had become fascinated by the antiquities of Egypt and managed to get a commission to go up the Nile in order to fetch down a colossal statue. His subsequent years in the country were spent in exploration and in the search for tombs and their contents. But that is another story. Here is one of his first adventures in Cairo.

"Going to the Citadel with Mr. Baghos, we had to pass through several of the principal streets, which are always crowded with people, and for this reason a stranger supposes the capital to be very populous; but except these streets and the bazars, the rest of the town is quite deserted, and a great number of falling houses and much rubbish are to be seen everywhere. We were mounted on our asses, the most convenient and only mode of travelling for Franks in that city. We met a soldier on horseback, who, when he came near, gave me such a blow with his staff upon my right leg, that I thought he had cut it in two. The staves of the Turks, which are like shovels, cut very sharp; and one of the corners, catching the calf of my leg, tore off a piece of flesh in a triangular form, two inches broad, and pretty deep. After this he swore two or three oaths at me, and went on as if nothing had happened. The blood ran out copiously; and instead of seeing the Bashaw, I was taken to the convent of Terasanta, as the nearest Christian place I could go to. It is to be remarked, that at this time, there was a great discontent among the soldiers against the Bashaw, for having given orders, that they should learn the European military evolutions; and, as I was in a Frank's dress, I suppose the fellow paid me for what he had learned of European fighting. From the convent I was taken home to my house in Boolak, where I remained under cure for thirty days, before I could stand on my legs. . . .
". . . When I recovered, I was presented to Mahomet Ali Bashaw, who received me very civilly. Seeing that I walked lamely, and being told the cause, he said, such accidents could not be avoided where there were troops."

The great authority upon life in Cairo is Lane, who went there in 1825, about the middle of Mehemet Aly's reign, and stayed many years, living as an Egyptian and making friends among all classes.

In 1836 he published his "Manners and Customs of the

Modern Egyptians " which, in spite of all changes is still the standard book.

Lane does not say much about the country people, but his descriptions of Turkish and Egyptian society in Cairo are most interesting, both as given in the " Manners and Customs " and in the notes to his edition of the Arabian Nights. As he shows, the Arabian Nights, though purporting to tell of Baghdad, were really Cairene stories of the Turkish period, written in Egyptian Arabic and giving the best possible idea of the manners of the time.

His book is so accessible that it is unnecessary to quote from it, but I should like to refer readers to his account of a Cairo house before they visit any of those actually surviving. There are still a good many of these, but the one most easy to see is known as the house of Gamal el Din, in a lane called the " Hōsh Kadam." This house was in a ruinous state and has been restored as a monument by the Comité de Conservation des Monuments Arabes. It is near the old main street, not very far from the Bab Zuweila, as we go towards the Mousky. We turn into a narrow lane and follow it, as it gets narrower and narrower, till the mushrabiya from the opposite windows actually touches above our heads. The massive house door, the vaulted ceiling of the entrance, the bench where the porter sat, the pretty courtyard inside, are exactly what we know from Pococke and Lane's descriptions. Upstairs is the open " mandara " where guests were received and within, a splendid " Ka'ah " or hall, cool, lofty and beautifully decorated with mosaic and marble panels. It has a recess for the orchestra, and above this, another similar recess, covered with mushrabiya work, where female musicians played and sang, or, it may be, the hareem could sometimes look on at the company in the hall below.

The remainder of the house, which has not been restored for show, probably contains another hall or halls for the hareem, but the smaller rooms are close and confined. Bedrooms, in the European sense, have only very lately come into use in Egyptian houses. The old way was to bring out quilts and unroll them anywhere that seemed cool and comfortable, or warm and stuffy, according to taste, and to make no fuss about dressing and undressing.

What strikes one about such a house is the extraordinary seclusion ; it is as much shut off from the world as if it were a prison. Its luxurious silence, its delicate ornament are guarded as if within a fortress. Anything might have happened there ; orgies of feasting, of lust, poisonings, mysterious disappearances.

A very good book upon the more modern life of Cairo is " Harems et Musulmanes " by " Niya Salima," a French lady who married a distinguished Turkish politician and wrote about 1900. Naturally, she mixed chiefly in the highest social circles and most of her friends were among the hareems of the Turkish Pashas, but she was very clear-sighted and took great pains to find out all she could about the middle- and lower-class hareems in Cairo. Her book is still very valuable, but she insists much upon the changes that were coming about at that time among the better classes ; these have now gone very much farther, and it is not too much to say that the life of the upper-class women in Cairo has totally altered. But " Niya Salima " knew the old ways as well as the new and gives us conversations between representatives of the two which show the conservative and the progressive point of view and all that is to be said for both.

The old ways were the ways that Lane tells of, with the reservation that he mostly speaks of the men and " Niya Salima " of the women. Both describe the large hospitality, the lavish expenditure at weddings, the slaves and children of slaves that hang around the hareems ; the amusements and the intrigues. And both insist much on the privacy within doors.

" When leave has been granted to a visitor " (says Lane) " it is customary for him, when he has to ascend to an upper apartment, to repeat several times some ejaculation, such as ' Permission,' or ' O Protector ' (that is, O protecting God) as he goes up, in order that any female of the family who may chance to be in the way, may have notice of his approach and either retire or veil herself."

Always the essential character of a Muslim household was seclusion. I close these few remarks on a very wide subject with a quotation from the Koran, which Lane gives as an illustration of this :

" O ye who have become believers, enter not any houses besides your own houses, until ye shall have asked leave, and saluted their inhabitants ; this will be better for you : peradventure ye will be admonished. And if ye find not in them any person, do ye return ; this will be more decent for you ; and God knoweth what ye do."

CHAPTER IX

SAKKARA

EVERYBODY enjoys the excursion to Sakkara, whether they are lovers of art, lovers of antiquities, or simply lovers of a picnic. For the first, it is the only place in the world where the oldest art is to be seen, not in a museum, but in its own surroundings. For the second, it is the cemetery of Memphis, full of relics of every period, since the great city had its beginning five thousand years ago ; while, for the third class of sight-seers, and indeed, for all the others too, it is delightful to get out into the country and see the crops and the animals, the birds, the funny little flocks of goats and donkeys and children, the laden camels swinging along the canal banks, and all the labour of the fields, changing with the changing seasons, but always good to look at.

There are several ways of getting to Sakkara and each of them has some special recommendation. One may go by train to Bedrashein and then by donkey or sand-cart, past the mounds of Memphis and the remains of the great temple of Ptah. Two colossal statues and a sphinx of Rameses II which stood in the precincts are still there, and very beautiful they look among the palm trees, but it is very doubtful whether any part of the more ancient buildings will ever come to light, for the water-level has risen since the Old Empire and excavation on this site is most difficult and expensive.

Or one may go from the Pyramids, across the desert, and see on the way, the Sun temple of Abu Ghurab and the Pyramids of Abusir, all of which are extremely interesting and well worth a visit.

Or one may drive straight from Cairo to Sakkara by motor-car. There are advantages and drawbacks about all these routes, but there is no doubt that if one has only a single day to give, much the most sensible way is to go by motor. The serious drawback to the first two mentioned is, that the getting there takes so long and involves so much fatigue that not enough time is left to see even the very best things at Sakkara, and Sakkara is far more important than any of the others.

Many people, tired and dazzled by the glare and the jolting of the ride, wander into the tombs for a few minutes, see nothing, and only remember Sakkara by the huge, dark vaults of the Serapeum. The Serapeum is very impressive, but it has nothing to do with early art, while it is just for the early art and the light that it throws on early life that Sakkara stands out pre-eminent.

The great centre of it all is the Step Pyramid, and the recent discoveries within the area of its enclosure are very startling. The funerary chapels laid bare during the last two seasons by Mr. C. M. Firth will cause the early chapters of the history of art and architecture to be rewritten ; not only for Egypt, but for the world.

At present these things are only in course of excavation ; without doubt more surprises await the further digging which must be done before the whole extent is explored. Problems have arisen which may be solved by later discoveries, and explanations may be made just now with apparent confidence, which may afterwards prove to have been ill-founded. So I enter on the description of these strange and novel buildings with the utmost diffidence ; yet, some description I must give ; all the more that little will appear in guide-books for some time to come and that the accounts given in newspapers only serve to call attention to the fact that discoveries have been made. No cursory reading of a paragraph or glance at a photograph will give any idea of what these things mean.

For, let there be no mistake about it, they are difficult. Sakkara was difficult enough without this ; a cemetery that lasted for more than three thousand years and contained millions of tombs, rich and poor, which altered in style with

PLATE VII

A THIRD DYNASTY PYRAMID TEMPLE AT SAKKARA

every age that passed, was bound to offer many puzzles and perplexities. And now, in addition to all this, these newly discovered buildings round the Step Pyramid, and undoubtedly of the same early date, upset all that one ever learned about the beginnings of architecture.

When the Step Pyramid was built, it stood alone. It was the first pyramid and has always been accounted the oldest stone building in the world. It looked down upon a group of brick tombs to the north, otherwise there was nothing round it but the barren desert. (Readers interested in the development of the tombs and pyramids are referred to my own book on " Egyptian History and Art.")

Zoser, or Neterkhet, the king who built it, made a large enclosure wall, which is still recognizable ; an oblong, close to the pyramid on the east and west sides, but stretching a considerable distance to north and south. The entrance was on the north, by a long and steep stairway descending into the rock. Succeeding pyramid builders followed this precedent of entering from the north, and always built their temples on the east side, but Neterkhet's temple seems to have been on a totally different plan and to have spread over a large portion of the whole enclosure. It is much destroyed, but later discoveries may explain some of its features.

Near the north-east corner of the pyramid, inside the great enclosure wall, are two mounds which have long been observed, and supposed to be the burying-places of some of the Royal family. This they certainly were, but now that they have been excavated, they are found to contain chapels of a perfectly new type of building. The masonry is of small blocks of limestone, beautifully dressed and fitted together. The façade is three-sided ; a sort of open courtyard, with the doorway to the tomb chapel in the middle of the north wall. On either side of the door are two engaged, fluted, limestone columns ; at the end of the wall is a pattern in relief, perhaps imitating papyrus stems, while the east and west walls are decorated with engaged columns of plain stone (Plate VII).

The illustration shows how marvellously Greek the place looks, but the appearance of it is positively staggering, when one actually sees the cream-toned limestone and the slender fluting of the pillars under the radiant blue sky of Egypt.

Could it be, could it, after all, possibly be a sixth-century Greek building ? No. It is as certain as anything can be that it is of the age of the pyramid. But whether this lovely work can by any possibility be the oldest building in stone is another matter, and one can really no longer believe in that. Still, all the signs about it show that all, or almost all of it, was dressed down by flint tools. So many unfinished or rejected blocks have been found that it is pretty clear how the work was done. Round holes about three inches across and two deep were drilled close together over the surface of the stone, the ridges left were then chipped away and the block dressed smooth with stone and sand. The same size of flint drill scooped out the flutings of the columns : a primitive method, but the regularity and beauty of the work would not shame a Doric temple.

There are three chapels of this description, probably belonging to the wives of the king. These chapels cannot have been covered by the sand until a comparatively late date, for there are numbers of graffiti on them scribbled by visitors from the Eighteenth Dynasty (*circ.* 1,500 B.C.) down to 600 B.C., which have all been deciphered, though not yet published. I understand that most of them express the admiration of the writers for the beauty of the monuments, but that one of them consists of a long complaint against the people who wrote their names and comments ; not, as we should expect, from any feeling that it was out of place to write little modern tags upon so fine and ancient a building, but that "the writing was so bad, it might have been that of women !"

The latest of these inscriptions is dated to the Saitic period, (sixth century B.C.), when some Greeks had already come to Egypt. The possibility has been suggested that these Greeks saw and carried away the idea of the fluted pillars, and that here at Sakkara may be the origin of the Doric column. I cannot venture to hold any opinion about this, but the idea is fascinating and ingenious.

Southwards, still within the pyramid enclosure, is a long

line of other buildings, of a novel and very remarkable design. These probably formed part of the temple precincts. The chapels, or whatever they may have been, adjoin one another, like a row of cottages, with a stair at one or two points, to an upper story. The beautiful masonry is the same and there are fluted columns in the decoration, similar to, but smaller than those in the queens' tombs.

Both orders of chapels appear to have had an upper storey, and so much of the dressed and fluted stone remains that Mr. Firth hopes to be able to rebuild a small part as it originally must have been. As yet, however, the stones are lying on the ground as they were found, and it will take the most painstaking labour to get the pieces into place. There is no guide to go by except size and shape, for nothing like this was ever seen before.

And this is not the end of the astonishing novelties. At the end of this row of buildings, we find that on the western side, instead of a sharp angle, the wall is rounded like a Roman bastion, a feature absolutely unknown in ancient Egypt hitherto. The entire character seems to be derived directly from construction in wood, but it is not possible, without entering too much into technical detail, to describe the peculiarities of design. No contemporary inscription is on any of those buildings.

The solitary bit of writing that has yet been found is on the base of the king's statue, which was built into a little shrine or " serdab," at the north-east corner of the pyramid, near the chapels first described.

It was completely enclosed within its walls, but in the northern one were two little peep-holes, through which one could see the king sitting inside. The statue bears his name and titles in good hieroglyphs of a rather archaic form and his dress is of a peculiar design, only hitherto known on an ancient ivory statuette. Instead of the usual Old Empire " kilt," he wears a long cloak, tightly wrapped round him, but leaving a bit of the shoulder bare. The type of face raises another point. It is totally different from the well-known features of the Fourth Dynasty statues, like Chephren and Mycerinus, but it is very much like something else. Fortunately, two or three other heads of the same style of work have already been found in the course of these excavations, so there is more than one factor to go on. It is far too early to say anything with certainty ; indeed, certainty may still be far off, but these sculptures seem to lend support to a theory to which I have always had some leanings.

In the Cairo Museum there is a strange group of colossal figures in black granite, which were found at Tanis in the Delta, and used to be called the " Hyksos statues." It was very natural to ascribe them to the Hyksos, partly because they did not look like anything that was known elsewhere, and no one knows anything about the Hyksos ; but with the stronger reasons that Tanis was the Hyksos capital, and the oldest of the many cartouches with which they are inscribed is that of a Hyksos king. But Tanis was a flourishing city long before the Hyksos ; moreover, it has been acutely observed that even this oldest cartouche was inscribed above something still more ancient. The possibility was then pointed out that all the group might be surviving specimens of the archaic art of northern Egypt. It seems to me that the striking resemblance of the Sakkara sculptures to these black statues bears out this idea in a surprising manner (*see* Egyptian Museum, Chapter IV).

Among the innumerable questions that all this gives rise to, the most important surely must be : What happened afterwards ? Why did this most ancient building, the characteristic of which was elegance rather than size, suddenly change to the art of the Fourth Dynasty ?

Why did these architectural forms occur in the very earliest times and never again ? Fluted columns or, rather, polygonal columns that appear fluted, are, it is true, known in Egypt, both in the Middle and in the New Empire, but what of the rounded bastion and the whole style of the façade as shown in our illustration ?

To the delicate beauty of the Sakkara building there succeeded the massive masonry of Cheops, the Granite Temple and the Chephren statue. Why was it ?

Though the world will never read clearly these pages of its early story, the effort to decipher them can never lose its fascination.

As to the other Old Empire tombs at Sakkara, which are among the most interesting things in Egypt, I feel it less necessary to write at any length, as some accounts of them are to be found in all guide-books. But, again, they are not easy to see.

I have sometimes thought, that if one could imagine a general destruction of the monuments of Egypt, out of which it was possible to save one thing only, that one thing would be the large room in the tomb of Ti. But for years I was in the habit of taking friends and friends of friends round to show them this tomb, and I can solemnly say that the majority of them saw very little in it. It is rather dark, the character of the reliefs is unfamiliar and the number of them bewildering. It is true that, if I had not pointed out things to them, they would have seen still less, but without some previous reading, it is hopeless for anyone to understand the meaning and purpose of the decoration, and without a good deal of time and patience, it is difficult to appreciate the extraordinary excellence of the work. Perhaps the artistic merit of these reliefs has had bare justice done to it, and that is the point I especially wish to emphasize. The first thing that stands out clearly is the excellent way the space is covered ; the beauty of pattern, irrespective of its meaning. When we begin to analyse this, we find that on each wall are several large figures, some seated, some standing, and that the space of wall in front of them is divided by horizontal lines. Between these lines are figures in action, which show rapid movement and an almost endless variety of attitudes. I suppose, however, that we ought to consider that in a way, their artistic excellence is incidental ; they were made, primarily, to tell their story and to be understood. It is a sort of extended writing and the big figure of Ti, presiding over each separate group of scenes, is like a capital letter indicating the beginning of a new sentence. The scenes in each group are continuous : the harvest scene, for instance, shows first the growing crop, then the cutting, binding the sheaves and lading them on donkeys, driving the donkeys home, piling the grain into temporary stacks ; then the winnowing, the threshing and lastly, the completed stack bound round with lotus stems.

The tomb of Ptahhotep is, like Ti, of the Fifth Dynasty, roughly about 2700 B.C., and, though smaller, it is equally fine. But when we turn from the two great chapels and look at the ordinary journeyman sort of work in the corridor and kitchen of the tomb of Ti, and the chapel of Akhthotep in the Ptahhotep tomb, it comes out very clearly that it was only the few great artists who could give life to their work, and that most people must have been content with something of a much more mechanical order.

The Sixth Dynasty tombs are not quite so good as the best of the Fifth, and the work is even more unequal, but there is a great variety of scenes in them and the observation of animal life is wonderful. In the tomb of Kagemna and in the first room in the tomb of Mera, are birds and fish, crocodiles and hippos, that are just as well done as it is possible to do them, and always, the artistic effect of the pattern is remarkably beautiful.

Round these Sixth Dynasty tombs the accumulated rubbish of thousands of years has recently been cleared away down to the original ground-level so that the tombs are now seen as they were when they were built, standing above-ground like rows of stone houses. This is one of the most thickly packed areas of the whole cemetery and one of the most difficult to excavate. The problems which confront the modern digger are different in many ways from what they used to be, for in Mariette's time, as in Schliemann's, the science of archæology was in its infancy. Mariette was a scholar and an enthusiast, and his discoveries were magnificent, but not nearly so much information was gained from them as would have been the case had photography been more advanced and the need of careful planning and note-taking been realized. No human being, moreover, could have adequately overlooked Mariette's *corvée* of 500 or 1,000 men. It is unfortunately certain that a great deal of material must have been destroyed and a great deal more passed unobserved.

The consequence is that the whole of this vast site has to be dug over again, and that, in the process, a large amount of rubbish will have to be cleared away in which nothing can be found ; it being merely the filling of one tomb shaft, dug out by Mariette and dumped upon another.

It is not uncommon for the excavator to spend days getting down to the bottom of a shaft, only to find there scraps of a French newspaper ! But it is not only Mariette and his *corvée* who may have been beforehand in opening any tomb. From the earliest times the steady occupation of a large part of the population was tomb robbing. There was always jewellery in the rich tombs and I do not think that any people have been able to resist digging up their ancestors if there was a lot of gold to be got off them. At all events, in every generation, there have been some who had no scruples. I am afraid the case looks very black against the Egyptian undertakers, who knew just how and where the tomb was blocked and what was worth the taking out. On the very rare occasions that I have seen an unplundered tomb found, it contained no jewellery, and there is little doubt that was the reason why it had been left alone.

This area round the pyramid of Teta and the Sixth Dynasty tombs now looks like a crater, with great walls of rubbish overhanging it. There are burials of every age ; of the Roman period at the top, below these, late Egyptians, then not quite such late Egyptians, then remains of fine chapels of the New Empire, with good sculptured reliefs and deep shafts sunk through the rubbish to the rock underneath, then shafts of Middle Empire tombs, with little chambers at the foot, filled with wooden model figures, then, really down on the rock, brick "mastaba" tombs of the Old Empire, sometimes containing a good statue or two, and faded paintings on the walls. If the place had been undisturbed, it would have been easy and very instructive to shave off layer by layer of this mass of remains, but actually, the condition rather reminded one of a pudding stirred up with a fork.

Everything has been turned over by robbers or by previous excavators, so everything found has to be considered separately, by the evidence it contains within itself, such as the shape of coffins, the style of inscriptions, the objects, or lack of objects that accompany any burial. It is extremely well worth doing, for the amount of information to be obtained· even from such a disturbed excavation as this, is quite surprising, but it requires experience, time and much patience.

Of the later Sakkara monuments, the Serapeum and the " Persian " tombs, it is needless to write, for little can be added to the guide-book information ; indeed, little can be described that cannot equally well be seen by the visitor for himself.

They are very impressive and very gloomy ; as far away from the joyous and vivid art of the Old Empire as they are from our own. That is true of their age also. The interval of two and a half millenniums that passed between the building of the Step Pyramid and the burial of the Apis bulls in their colossal granite coffins within the dark galleries of the Serapeum is as long as that which separates the Apis burials from the present day.

It is an imposing place and must be seen, but I do not think anyone ever wants to see it more than once ; whereas, no one can ever look often enough at the harvesting and hunting in the tomb of Ti or at Ptahhotep's fighting boatmen.

CHAPTER X

DESERT TRAVEL

IT is an undoubted fact that, to many people who live among the complicated conveniences of the present day, the best possible holiday is to get away from them all and have neither telephones nor wireless, neither business nor parties to trouble about, but to get down to the necessaries of life and be free to wander where they will.

No place can be better than the Egyptian desert for such a trip ; good weather for the greater part of the year, wonderful fresh air, excellent transport and freedom to go exploring and to pitch the tent where fancy dictates. Then there is the much-talked-of " fascination and mystery of the desert." It is there, sure enough ; no doubt about it : the sunrises and sunsets, the outgoings of the morning and the evening, the nights of pearly moonlight or clear, starry darkness, the solitude, the great silence and the wide spaces. The fascination is there ; it is strong ; yet, I think it is obvious. It grips one at the first. Of the many beautiful descriptions of it by gifted writers, it seems to me that the best are written after just a glimpse of it ; a few days in a tent, a few nights under the stars. I do not think the fascination lasts.

It is not the heat, nor the glare, nor the sandstorms, nor even the solitude, that become oppressive after a time ; it is the utter deadness and the howling of the wind. There are, it is true, some rare souls that go off time and again for long treks of lonely months and do not seem to weary of it. I humbly own that I am not of these. After many years of life on the desert edge, I feel that I have had as much as I can bear of it as a place for a permanent home. I have not come

117

to hate it, as some do. There is nothing I enjoy more than days or weeks or even months in the desert, but the wind and the awful monotony have entered into my soul and I am glad not to have to live there any longer. Thankful, too, that our home was always on the edge of the cultivation, and not right out in the wilderness, for we had a great view over the green land, with villages and palms, and across the winding river to a stretch of sand leading up to the line of high cliffs where the eastern desert breaks down into the Nile Valley. Round about us were cemeteries of old Egyptians, buried thousands of years ago ; rather dismal neighbours, one might have thought, but they never depressed us much. Indeed, I came to feel them companionable, compared with the barrenness beyond, for they, at least, were once alive, and, by all accounts, enjoyed it very much. Behind us, long lines of desert sloped slowly upwards and westwards, to infinity. This was the typical landscape, whether seen from the temporary shelter of a tent, a tomb, or, as it was later, from the balcony of a good stone house. The cliffs might be higher and steeper, the low desert between our camping ground and the cultivation might be wider in one place than another, but all over Upper Egypt, the character of the scenery is much the same.

Of all these different dwelling places, give me, for choice, if for not too long a time, a good tomb. It is sometimes objected to, by those unacquainted with the merits of a tomb as a place to live in, on the ground that, as one is sure to spend a great deal of time there eventually, it is a mistake to begin too soon. But it has so many recommendations that one gets over that point of view. It is warm in cold weather, very fairly cool when it is hot ; it is silent and still ; the wind does not blow one's possessions about, it is generally pretty well lighted by a door and sometimes a window, for it is hardly necessary to say that I am not speaking of the funeral vault, the place where the coffin is, but of the tomb chapel above, where the services were held. In Upper Egypt, these are generally hollowed out of the rock, like caves, and a long row of them together can accommodate quite a large household. The shafts, at the bottom of which the real burial is, sometimes still gape in the floor and one has to be careful not to fall in, but this is almost the only drawback.

Mud huts, if run up cheaply, are probably the worst kind of abode, but if well built, they approach the standards of a simple house and then can be lived in indefinitely.

Tents, unless really large and well made, are comfortless places for a long stay, but for a short camping trip they are the only possible thing. And how cheerful and cosy it is to come in at the end of a long day in the open air, to find the tents pitched, tea ready and everything looking just as it did in the morning, when the camp was struck miles away! Then the quiet night and the sharp, chilly morning air, breakfast, packing, the camels gurgling as each package is fastened on their unwilling backs; how soon it grows familiar, and how delightful it is!

The advent of the motor-car has changed desert travelling, as it has changed so much else. It is quite possible to visit many places and to get a very good idea of desert scenery from expeditions in a motor, but it is not the real thing at all. To taste the joy of camping, we must be self-contained and wander slowly, carrying our food and shelter, and, if need be, our water supply with us. It is only so that we can achieve complete independence.

But some motor trips round Cairo are very pleasant and easy to manage. Suez can be reached in a day by car, but this is not advisable to attempt without preliminary inquiry, as sometimes the track gets torn up by rainstorms and travellers may be seriously delayed. For the first part of the way, however, the going is usually good. Starting from Heliopolis, the newest and northernmost of Cairo suburbs, the road is excellent for some distance, and once the long slope has been climbed, the scenery becomes interesting. There are typical wadys of the Eastern desert to be crossed, full of the regular desert vegetation of low scrub and brushwood, brown or green according to the season. Near the highest point is a palace, built there out in the desert by one of the Khedives for a Bedouin wife. But it was hardly inhabited at all and is now falling into the dreary dilapidation of a modern ruin.

Another very attractive expedition is to Wady Hof, which can be done either by car all the way, or by train to Heluan and thence by donkey. It is one of the long wadys which scar the face of the eastern desert, and is perhaps the finest in this part of Egypt, for the hills are high and in some places the cliffs rise to sheer precipices above the wady floor. In heavy rain, a torrent rushes along the dry river-bed and is swelled by short-lived tributaries from every rocky gorge. Generally it is all over in a day, but the moisture left behind gives life to numberless little seeds which spring up among the sand and gravel. Curious, inconspicuous little flowers they are, which blossom there after the rain. At one place, where water gathers in a deep, round cavity, there are even tiny fronds of maidenhair fern, nestling in the clefts of the rock.

A motor cannot get down into the Wady, but walkers can leave the car and explore the side wadys which debouch on the main one, or climb some one of the surrounding heights and get wide views of the eastern desert and of the Nile Valley. It is a charming place for a picnic ; beautiful air, quiet ; fine rocky scenery and plenty of brushwood to kindle a fire and boil the kettle.

The nearest bit of desert to Cairo is the plateau behind the Citadel, but it is not accessible by motor. It makes a delightful donkey ride or a long walk ; in fact the view from the top, near the old mosque of Gayushi, is much finer than the famous prospect from the Citadel.

For those who want a real camping tour, the choice is end-less ; the desert is everywhere, up and down the length of Egypt. Determining factors must be personal taste, the time and money to be expended, and the season of the year. In winter, there is no doubt that Upper Egypt should be chosen as, for grandeur of scenery and practical certainty of weather, it is preferable to any other place.

Very fine tours can be taken from Luxor, where camels and tents can be hired. The most adventurous, likewise the most expensive, of these starts from Keneh and goes up the Wady Keneh to the porphyry quarries in the eastern desert, which lie among splendid mountain scenery. These quarries were worked in Roman times and never before nor since. The old Egyptians did not work this stone, and since Roman times, nobody has ever faced the difficulty and expense of the transport of the blocks and the maintenance of a large number of workmen in so remote a spot. But all the fine porphyry basins, statues and columns which we see in Italian churches came from here and were conveyed from these quarries to Rome and Constantinople for the Imperial palaces and State buildings.

The quarry workings and the houses of the workmen remain as they were left in the early centuries of the Christian era, while all the stations and watering-places used by the trains of camels that carried the food and brought away the stone are still to be seen and are used by the few travellers of the present day.

Another very interesting and less difficult trip is across the pass from Keneh to the Red Sea, passing through the quarries of Hammamat, which were much worked in Old Egyptian times. On the rocks are many inscriptions, dating from the Old Empire onwards. (A good account of both these expeditions is given in Weigall's " Travels in the Egyptian Desert.")

The Hammamat road ends at the port of Kosseir. It is now often done by motor, as the phosphate mines and oil workings on the Red Sea Coast are easier of access from Keneh than from any other point in Egypt, and the gradients are easy. Kosseir used to be of great importance for the pilgrims to Mecca. They crossed the hundred miles from Keneh by camels supplied by the Ababdeh Arabs, and, from Kosseir, went by boat to Jeddah. Kosseir is a completely waterless spot, but there has been a distilling plant there for a long time, so supplies can be replenished for a camel party. How the great company of pilgrims were provided for in old times, it is difficult to understand.

A long trip of this kind, where all the water has to be carried, is, inevitably, a complicated and expensive way of going about, but it is a wonderful experience for those who can manage it.

The sort of camping which I have had most opportunity of doing, is simply moving along the desert edge in search of cemeteries, and even without any special predilection for that engaging pursuit, very pleasant expeditions may be made in this way, which is much less expensive than the distant tours. Water is always within reach ; milk, eggs and fowls can be got in any village ; on market days there is meat, and in the larger towns of Upper Egypt, most excellent bread. This is the best way of seeing some of the more inaccessible antiquity sites, like El Kab and Tell el Amarna and of visiting many beautiful bits of rock scenery in the Thebaid.

In spring or in the early winter, the Fayum makes an attractive desert trip. A very good plan is to spend a few days camping at Sakkara, so as to see the place more thoroughly than can be done by excursions from Cairo, and then to cross the strip of desert, obtaining on the way a splendid view over the richly cultivated Fayum, the Birket Karun and the distant Libyan desert. The lake is much shrunken from what it was in very ancient days, when it covered almost the whole of the present province of the Fayum. It is fed by the Bahr Yusuf, which takes off from the Nile at Assiut and flows down near the Western desert till it comes to an end in the Fayum oasis. There used to be no regular outflow to the Nile, but in the time of high flood the water made a channel for itself. By a great achievement of irrigation, the Middle Empire engineers, about 2000 B.C., reclaimed part of this land from the lake and put regulating sluices on the Bahr Yusuf and on the outflow to the Nile. But it was not until Ptolemaic times that the great scheme was undertaken which converted most of the lake and its surrounding marshes into one of the most fertile provinces of Egypt. It was largely inhabited by Greeks, for grants of land were given by the Ptolemies to Greek mercenaries when they left military service, to encourage them to settle in Egypt. Plate VIII is probably a portrait of one of them. It is due to this colony that the enormous masses of papyri which have been found

PLATE VIII

PORTRAIT FROM COFFIN FOUND IN THE FAYUM
(circ. 120 A.D.)

in the rubbish heaps of these old towns and villages are nearly all written in Greek. These papyri are the most notable things that the Fayum sites have yielded, for, on the whole, the antiquities of the Fayum are not very interesting, though the place, in itself, is attractive. But beyond the lake, far out on the desert, remarkable fossil remains have been found of very early mammals, some of which are in the Geological Museum at Cairo ; others in the Museum of Natural History at S. Kensington. It seems certain that further discoveries of this nature await the explorer.

The Western desert is very monotonous in this part ; the cliffs are low and there are no rocky wadys to vary the scenery ; a few days of it will suffice for most people. The eastern side of the valley is more interesting, and a short round of one or two days, just enough to give one some idea of it, can be made from Cairo.

I did this one April, starting from Heliopolis in a hot wind and wondering why we had been foolish enough to go. For two or three hours up the long slope the unpleasant conditions lasted, but after passing the Petrified forest and crossing the first wady, the wind dropped, then veered to the north and a beautiful evening followed. It was dark when we reached the camping place in the Wady Degla, a wide valley thickly overgrown with low bushes, where there was a well and an old Bedouin with a goat or two, who picked up a scanty living by gathering the pollen from the fragrant desert plants for the bazaars in Cairo. It was an ideal camping ground, with plenty of brushwood for the fires, and the camel men kept up a merry blaze all through the night. Next day we crossed the wady and went on for hours on hard, high desert, with range upon range fading into faintest blue on the far horizon, till, in the late afternoon we descended into the Wady Hof and came down upon Heluan.

In early summer the best camping trip that could be taken is to the west of Alexandria, to the district described in the first chapter, round the Menas Monastery and the lighthouse of Abusir. A few days in tents beside that turquoise sea, with the ruins to explore and the strange landscape to enjoy,

would make a most delightful holiday. There is, after all,
no way of seeing a country like walking or riding over it.
That, and the delicious sense of freedom which is given by
having no cares about baggage or lodgings or trains is secured
in perfection by desert travel. The air is like champagne,
light and stimulating. Perhaps on a winter morning, we may
feel that the champagne is rather too much iced, but the midday sun is powerful and the active exercise we take keeps off
any real suffering from cold.

If we have a little Arabic and time to make friends, a good
deal of pleasant companionship is sometimes to be had with
our travelling companions, who are the cheeriest of neighbours in the nightly camps. After a long day's work, they
are ready to amuse themselves in the evenings with matches
at singlestick, story telling, or, on certain festive occasions,
with what is known as a " zikr." This is a sort of religious
country dance, of a most vigorous and exhausting character,
something like the ritual of the dancing dervishes. I have
not much experience of the genuine Bedouin, but many of the
Upper Egypt fellahin, the class of Egyptian with whom I
am best acquainted, are half or more than half Arab in blood,
and delight in living on the desert, whereas the regular village
people are afraid of it. Even where we generally lived, about
a mile out from the cultivation, it was very difficult to get
donkeys to bring anyone up after dark and nobody would
think of getting a telegram or letter delivered until the morning. The fellahin are terrified to go about on the desert
because of " afreets " and the desert people are afraid to go
about the cultivation because of robbers and night watchmen,
who are very casual about letting off their guns. On the
other hand, our workmen who lived near us on the desert,
didn't seem to have the slightest fear of " afreets." Their
fears were all for the human bad characters who were supposed
to infest the cultivated land, so, if we did happen to be out
late, when we got back on to the sand, there was a sigh of
relief, and " Now, O Sitt, there is nothing to fear."

One of the camel men whom my husband used to employ
was a man whose conversation was a perpetual entertainment.

He was far from being an estimable character, in fact he was a consummate intriguer and was suspected of being in league with the worst criminals in the neighbourhood, but he served us well and listening to him was like hearing a chapter from the Arabian Nights. We observed that one of his numerous brothers seemed to be very much better off than the rest of the family and lived in quite a different style. When we came to know the man and the place better, we inquired as to the reason of this and were told the following story. I ought to say that our friend, in addition to his other undesirable qualities, was a champion liar, but I don't think there was any cause to doubt the main facts of this narrative, which, at all events, is characteristic and credible.

" Your Excellency knows that we are five brothers and that our father looked after the property belonging to M. Pasha (naming a noted Turkish soldier and official) who owned the land round our village. He was very kind to all our family and liked to come out to the desert to ride and to shoot duck on the ponds near by. Then he used to come and have dinner in our house and said that he was glad to get away from his palace in Cairo and be with good people in the country. Also, Your Excellency, his wife ruled the house in Cairo and made trouble for him and he came to find peace among us. One day that he came, he was in very bad spirits and took no pleasure in his hunting. When my father asked him what ailed him, he sighed and said, ' I will tell thee, O Abdullah. My wife is making my life a burden to me because of a gâria (white slave girl) of whom she has become jealous. Now the girl is a good girl and I wish her well and would not have her ill-treated. At the same time, I cannot bear my life as it is and I have determined to give her in marriage. And I will give with her as a dowry two acres of land and sufficient stock of household furniture. Now, as there are none of all my servants whom I prize as I do you and your sons, I have said to myself that I will tell you of this and I will ask if one of your sons will take her to wife.' And we all five arose as one man and said with one voice : ' I will take her to wife.' ' Very good,' said the Pasha, ' then I will give her to one of you, but which it shall be, she must choose for herself.' And so he appointed a day for us to go to his palace in Cairo, and there we walked through the courtyard of the hareem, one after the other, she looking down at us from a window. And when we had all passed, she said ' I will take Aly.' And when she came here, she had with her two boat-loads of copper basins and other things for the house, jewellery, and many fine clothes."

There is another story in which our camel-hiring friend figures which I should like to tell once more, but have some hesitation, for it has been received with uniform disbelief varying from the derisive jeers of intimates to the politely veiled incredulity of acquaintances.

And yet it is quite a true tale, and may, perhaps be accepted by a wider public !

When one lived on the edge of the desert, some six miles from a station, before the days of motor-cars, the best way of getting about and the only way of getting goods from the market, was on donkey back, in the good old-fashioned style. We had three donkeys. Two of them came with us from a camp farther south, and were fine, upstanding beasts, with high tempers and rapid paces, but the third was smaller, older, much gentler and ambled along with a pleasant, quiet gait. He was purchased locally and was much objected to by the two already in possession, who, though they fought furiously with each other, would not suffer any strange donkey and snapped vigorously at any attempt to come alongside them in a ride. However, we were well enough pleased with them all. But the beginning of trouble was that one day, the little donkey seemed unable to keep on the path and kept diverging to the right and left without any visible provocation from the other two. Next day, it was worse, for it nearly precipitated its rider into a tomb shaft and it was clearly time to make a medical examination. The result was deplorable ; the poor little beast had gone totally blind. This was really a serious mishap, for what can anyone do with a blind donkey ? Humanity forbade its being shot, yet it may well be that time would have deadened our feelings, and that would have been its ultimate fate, for no hope of recovery was held out to us. The Vet. smiled patronizingly, the villagers recommended mysterious compounds of mummy and other drugs, but everybody was helpless.

Day after day we tested the donkey by passing a candle before his eyes, but never was there a sign of returning sight ; eye washes were tried, and such of the suggested prescriptions as seemed at all practicable and not too ancient Egyptian. The camel man advanced an idea with great seriousness, which did not commend itself, though we listened attentively. This was it.

" Is it not well known that, when any part is ill, the sure way to cure it is to raise up another pain in some other part of the body, as far away as it may be from the part that is suffering ? There was a man who had a cat that he was very fond of and the cat went blind. So the man knew that if the cat could have its tail cut off or wounded that the sight would return. And he brought a good bowl of milk and called the cat to it and as she was drinking, he took his knife and sliced the tail off. And the cat saw again as well as ever."

This seemed rather drastic to try on the chance, but we were much interested in the notion and spoke at table of it as a curious example of a counter-irritant. Whether we also spoke of it in the stable, I have never been able to recollect, but somebody surely must have done so ; or, did the other donkeys know better all the while ? Or, why was it that, the morning after we had been told of the cure of the cat, one of them had managed to work himself loose in the night, had gone for the little donkey and bitten off its tail ?

It was a horrid spectacle ; the tail was hanging by a tag of skin and the big teeth had made a rough and angry-looking wound, caked with clotted blood. But the little donkey did not seem much discomposed, and now comes the remarkable bit of the story. *It had recovered its sight.*

CHAPTER XI

CAIRO TO LUXOR: THE VILLAGES

THERE is generally a bustling crowd on the Upper Egypt platform of Cairo station on a winter evening, when the express is starting and the passengers are looking out their sleepers and bespeaking their dinners. The train carries them out of the big, light station into the night and, in the bright warm morning deposits them at Luxor. Nothing could be more comfortable or more commonplace. Yet it is not easy to do better. The river trip, when the boat is not too full and the weather not too cold, does give the traveller a perfectly restful time and the opportunity of seeing many very interesting places. As a rest it is ideal ; there is always something to look at, for, though the country is monotonous, the river life is fascinating to watch. The white-sailed boats, the birds, the shadoofs laboriously lifting the water to the fields, the changing lights, the tints of sunsets, are endlessly delightful. The drawbacks to the steamer trip are that too short time is given to see Luxor properly, and that it is difficult to go about quietly by oneself. A private steamer is, of course, much the best, but this is a counsel of perfection and far out of most people's reach. The dahabieh, which used to be universal until about forty years ago, has gradually gone out of use since the railway was made and the good hotels at Luxor and Assuan came into being. Also the delays are more troublesome than formerly, owing to the Barrages at Assiout and Esna. There is nothing whatever to prevent anybody having a dahabieh now, for there are plenty to be hired, but apparently the modern traveller is in too great a hurry to care for it. And it was, needless to say, inevitable that, wherever there was a place one particularly wanted to stay, such a good wind was blowing that it required struggles to persuade the captain to stop ; conversely when the boat was held up by a bad wind, it was invariably on a sandbank or at some point absolutely without interest. For all that, with plenty of time and very congenial company, it must be a beautiful way to spend a winter and the best possible means of seeing some aspects of the country.

But, however one goes, by train or by the Nile, one never touches the life of Egypt. In rides through the cultivation one sees and comes to know the varying crops in the fields and the unchanging customs of the people, but even with some knowledge of the language, it is very difficult to get below the surface, or even to interpret that surface aright. The villages have not changed as Cairo has changed, and though there is much more money about than there used to be and the well-to-do people are better housed, the manner of life is much the same as it was long ago. The typical village is a poor-looking place enough ; pretty at a distance with palm groves and fruit trees surrounding it, but within the cluster of houses are tortuous lanes, crowded with people and swarming with flies. No room for wheeled traffic, but strings of camels take up the width of the street, swinging their spreading loads so that pedestrians are driven into open doorways or flattened out against the walls. In an open space will often be a few black Bedouin tents, inhabited by squatters, who come to mend pots and pans and disappear again into the desert. The butcher sets up a tripod in any widening of the roadway, and from it there dangles, according to the time of day, the whole or portions of the carcass of a buffalo or a goat ; in an open booth are a few tins and some rolls of coloured cotton, but the Greek, always present in the larger places, has not yet opened a store in the remoter villages.

The threshing mill is a great resort for men and women, and there is usually at least one handloom in the village, where the thread spun by the men is woven into material for their ample cloaks. A mosque or two there will be, but rarely

a school. The people are not very friendly at first, but that
soon wears off, and if one could face the discomfort and the
vermin and take time and trouble to be kind to the women
and children and doctor them, the whole village would come
round in no time and some kind of affection would be called
out. There is plenty to do for the poor things, for their
babies come with appalling frequency and die nearly as fast,
but when one sees how they are brought up, the wonder is
rather that any of them live than that many of them die.
I don't think it would really be of much use, for old habits
are deeply ingrained, especially the belief in magical practices,
and the distrust of Christians is pretty firmly rooted, yet it
gives qualms of conscience sometimes, when one has had the
chances I have had, that one had done so little for them.
But one would have to be so full of sympathy and enthusiasm
as only to think of their needs and how to relieve them ; or
else so genuinely benevolent that one would carry on, undis-
couraged by many disillusionments and disappointments.

I think Belzoni's account of the Egyptian character, though
far from sympathetic, is worth quoting.

" A traveller who has all the accommodation possible, and
nothing to do with these people but in passing, can never
judge of their ideas, their system of conduct and their rapa-
cious manners ; for in the little interval and the limited business he has to conduct with them, they do not appear to be
the people they really are. Some travellers even receive
civilities, with which they are mightily pleased ; without
having time to discover, that the very persons whom they
suppose to be naturally civil, are only so to serve their own
interested views. They pass on, and in their journal of
remarks just say, that they were received civilly at such and
such a place.   But let a traveller deal with them in any trans-
action where their interest is concerned, and where the execution of any undertaking is required, and he will soon find
that in every point they are the most cheating people on earth.
A traveller passing by a village stops his bark for an hour or
two : what good people he finds. Some bring him a small
basket of dates, others a few eggs, another some bread and
milk ; with which he is so pleased that he immediately gives

them five or perhaps ten times more than the worth of what he receives, without being aware, that it is through such an expectation they bring him these things, but exclaims that in Europe they do not treat a stranger so civilly.   But let him take the smallest of these presents without giving anything in return or even no more than it is worth, they will not fail to murmur at him.   If he give only double the price, they have the art of returning the money with scorn and contempt, in order to shame him to give more ; and if he take the money returned, or give them nothing from the beginning, he must not expect that they will let him go away without paying for what they brought him.   All this is unknown to a traveller merely passing by, for there is no one in this character, who would be so mean as to accept anything, without returning double or treble its value.   From these trifles it may be presumed what they are in all their dealings : to-night one word for such a thing, to-morrow another ; their intrigues are beyond description ; they have the art of making one thing appear like another so well, that it is very difficult to avoid falling into their trap.

" There are two extremes in travellers.   One who has just arrived, has never before been in the country, and of course has no knowledge of customs and things, cannot see a fourth of what he should see : the other is so thoroughly initiated into their customs and manners, that those which shock at first sight, lose their effect on him ; he almost forgets his own ways, and does not reckon anything he beholds extraordinary or worth attention, though perhaps even of the greatest consequence."

This is true enough, but not the whole truth.   Egyptians are not all alike, any more than other people, and most of us who have lived long in the country have found friendly feelings and faithful service, the memory of which will not pass away from either side.

We had extremely pleasant relations with a wealthy family in one of the villages near where we lived.   The Bey himself was a cultivated gentleman of the old school, a student of El Azhar and a man of considerable influence in the district.

He had a house in Cairo and a wife and family there, but also a wife and family at his country estate.   It was the

country hareem that I knew best and they were simple people,
really just well-to-do fellahin, but the town lady was of quite a
different class, dressed well, went out daily in a carriage and,
on the rare occasions of her visits to the village, found the
place so insufferably dull that she would not stand it for more
than a week at a time. I do not wonder. She is of the new
world and they are of the old. The family of the country
wife were all daughters and they led the typical life of a well-
ordered country hareem. They are never out of doors, they
cannot read, they do not sew, they have servants to do, or
rather to leave undone the housework ; in short, the emptiness
of their lives is awful. As a rule, they marry their cousins,
go to live in a house near by and stay there. It was only
after getting on rather confidential terms with one or two of
them that I learned that sometimes, when the Bey was not
at home, they would slip out in the evening and go round to
the old house.

My first introduction to the village was rather impressive.
Very soon after our arrival in the neighbourhood we were
asked to the wedding of one of the daughters. The festivities
went on for several days and I was, and still am, hazy as to
what stage of the celebrations we lighted on, but I dare say
the scene would have been much the same on any other of
the evenings. As we rode down from the quiet of the desert
we could see the glow and hear the hum of the great party
from a distance ; when we drew nearer to the blaze of light
that flamed at the far end of the village, a huge marquee
disclosed itself, gay inside with blue and red and hanging lamps.
It was full of men ; tarbooshed effendis in European dress,
dignified Egyptians in flowing robes of cloth and silk, peasants
in blue cotton galabiehs. The crowd of guests was far too
big for the tent and stretched outwards into the darkness,
where, under the palms, we could see the gleam of water from
a pond. There was a tight-rope performer, dancing girls,
singers, all from Cairo and the best obtainable, and there
was feasting for every one on the most lavish scale of hospitality. We were ushered through the crowd and welcomed by
the courteous host, who made us sit beside him on a divan

and pointed out the various amusements which were provided. It was very magnificent and very picturesque, but I felt singularly out of place, the one woman among those hundreds of men. I had expected things to be done as they had been at the Cairo weddings I had gone to, where the men stayed downstairs and had their entertainment and the women were upstairs in the hareem, where there was plenty going on, dancing, singing, supper and lively, free and easy talk. So I felt that the proper thing for me was to suggest that I should join the ladies, and I was a little surprised to see a shade of embarrassment pass over the Bey's countenance. However, he agreed at once, said he would conduct me to the hareem himself, but would first send word that we were coming. Then he led me away from the lighted tent into a dark lane from which we turned into the courtyard of a house. There we sat and waited for a light; the Bey talking to me with the utmost affability, but I feeling every minute more conscious that I must have done the wrong thing. After a lantern had been brought, out we went again into the dusty and darksome lane and up it, it seemed to me, for an interminable distance. I have grown familiar with the house and the lane since then, in many friendly visits and I realize that it is not so far from place to place as it appeared on that first evening; still, as there are several houses belonging to the family and the Bey's hareem is at the farthest end, I do not much wonder that I felt bewildered. Out of the lane at last, into a smaller, darker, courtyard than the first, waking up hens and geese, which squawked as we passed through, up a dirty staircase to a little landing from which one or two rooms opened. In one of the rooms, a small square box of a place, poorly lighted by one candle, with a bowl of incense smoking on the table, sat a girl, the bride, alone save for an older woman, I think her mother. The bride was a slim, graceful creature of seventeen or so dressed in rich white satin, a veil of tinsel and pink gauze falling over her long black plaits of hair, jewels on her neck and arms, paint and kohl upon her face. The mother had no wedding garment, so far as I could see, but indeed it was not easy to see what any of them wore, for,

10

at the sound of the Bey's cough as he followed me into the
room, both the women sprang from their seats, veiled themselves hurriedly and cowered in the corner. It was a well-
ordered Muslim household of the old school and this was
undoubtedly the correct way to receive the master of the
house. When I came to know them better, I understood
that that was all, but that night I was aghast and felt more
awkward and uncomfortable than has often been my lot.
It didn't make matters better when the Bey settled himself
beside me on the divan and began to make elaborate conversation in high Arabic, which, at the best of times, is too high
for me, and then seemed simply out of reach. I couldn't
understand him and could hardly stammer out a word of
courtesy in reply. I longed to speak to the two trembling
things in the corner, but there, too, I felt tongue-tied and could
only ask to be allowed to come again, when all the gaieties
were over. I paid many visits afterwards and became familiar
with the little courtyard and the poultry and very friendly
with the inmates, of whom there were far more than my
original two, indeed it was most difficult at first to find out
who was who, so many families lived together and there were
so many babies and servants that it was long before I was
able to place them all. With one or two of the older women,
and especially with the little bride, I came to have a measure
of intimacy, and on the rare occasions when I found her
alone, we used to have real human conversation. We soon
got past the regular routine of conventional remarks. Calls
in Egypt are generally interminably long, but make no serious
demands on one's powers of being agreeable, for all parties
can sit silent as long as they like, at intervals breaking out
with " We have indeed missed you," " You have honoured
us," " May God preserve you," and the like. But after
having run rapidly over these polite preliminaries, we used
to pass on to the weightier matters of maternity, past, present
and to come. That was the usual topic, as it must be in
every place where women have no outside interests, but it
was by no means the only one. We talked of the differences
of customs, the cost of housekeeping, histories of my visitors,

and sometimes, in rare bursts of confidence, I used to be told
of family feuds and scandals.

It is fair to say, that though the villages have not changed
much, things have improved since then.   The houses are
better and much airier and brighter, for great prosperity has
come to the well-to-do landowners, most of whom have either
built new houses or made large additions to the old ones.
But the life of the country hareem goes on much as it did,
and often when I see the charmingly dressed ladies in black
silk habaras going about Cairo in well-appointed motors, my
mind goes back to that first sight of a genuine country
house, the darkness and the squalor, and the girl bride, sitting
lonely, out of sight and sound of the great fantasía given in
her honour.

As to the fellahin women who work in the fields and have,
of course, much more liberty, I am afraid their lives are even
less enviable.   In a house such as I have been describing,
the lot of the women is, at least, secure.   Even if a woman
is divorced, she has her father's house open to her, she has
powerful protection against ill-treatment and a good chance
of making another marriage in her own class.   But the fellahin
girls are married very young ; any time after ten years old.
Legislation has lately been brought in to defer the age com-
pulsorily, but it is doubtful how it will work.   There is some
safeguard in the fact that the first marriage is nearly always
to a cousin, and so the girl remains more or less in her own
family, but divorce is so terribly common that conditions get
worse and worse for a woman the older she grows.

I quote a passage from " Niya Salima's " excellent book as
confirmation of this.

" La vie des musulmanes de la basse classe pourrait s'écrire
en un livre de trois ou quatre pages.   Sur la première, avec
des couleurs violentes, des jaunes aveuglantes et des rouges
pourpres, une image representerait la fête tapageuse
de la noce, seule journée vraiment heureuse de leur existence, et, sur chacune des feuilles suivantes, trois mots invari-
ables résumeraient toute leur histoire : mariage, maternité,
divorce."

Happily there are alleviations even to this woeful fate.
Youth and an open-air life count for a good deal and certainly
there is always gaiety and merriment among the girls. Some
of them, I am sure, find great amusement in the discharge
of certain pious duties. There are marriages, funerals, cir-
cumcisions, at which the whole village holds a fantasía, and
the women take a prominent part. At one village there was
a curious practice which gave immense enjoyment to the
youthful female part of the population. The village had a
reputation as having been the abode of a sheikh, whose
tomb stands at the foot of a steep sand slope at the desert
edge. Every Friday morning, when the men are at the
mosque, the women and girls gather at the top of this slope
and those desirous of motherhood carefully tuck up their
skirts round their legs and roll down to the little tomb. I
think it must be partly for fun, as quite small children do it
as well as the older ones and they, surely, are more concerned
with the romp of the moment than with the hope of maternity
in the future. They are shy of being overlooked and one
would not for the world, have them think they were being
watched, but after they got accustomed to our being in the
neighbourhood, I often used to pass by when the performance
was going on without their taking any notice of me. I was
curious to know whether the place was credited with peculiar
merits beyond the bounds of the village, so I made inquiries
of my friends who lived some distance away and was told
that certainly this was a holy sheikh and very efficacious.
They told me the proper ritual, which was to accompany or
precede the rolling downhill. There was a prescribed arrangement of the dress and then a little poem to be recited to the
sheikh and to a lady saint, also of the village, promising to
bring a sweet-scented bouquet to be offered at the shrine, if
all went well.

In somewhat striking contrast to the ordinary hareem is
the status of women who have independent means. They
retain possession of their property, unaffected by marriage
or divorce, and, so far as I have seen, they are excellently
well able to take care of it. Although they would not appear

before a man unveiled, they can hold their own with anybody in defending their rights, and frequently, they are quite unmistakably, the ruling partners in the house.   In the richer classes in Cairo, when the wife is often the owner of the house, her position is very strong, because then, in case of divorce, it is the husband who has to turn out.

It is most difficult for any outsider to know anything of the darker side of hareem life, or of village life altogether. Tragedies are not very rare ; of that much one is certain, but how can the outside world hear of things which the whole of the inhabitants conspire to conceal ?   Within the hareem no one has much business to know what goes on except the master of the house, and, supposing a daughter of his has " blackened the face of her father," all public opinion would be with him in inflicting the severest penalties.

Once, years ago, a tale was told which struck me so much that I wrote it down, recasting it a little to bring out the setting, which was in a part of Egypt I knew very well.   So the wording of the story is my own, but the outlines of it are exactly what we were told and I think it is remarkable enough to be worth repeating.   It was given to us as an instance of the frequent miscarriage of justice and the impossibility of Government officials getting to know the truth of things.

" Hassan Mahmoud was well satisfied with the business he had done.   He had been down as far as Assiout with a cargo, had been well paid and now had turned southwards with a fresh breeze blowing him up-stream.   His brother, Dahshur, a lad of fifteen or sixteen, was sitting forwards, mending linen, while Hassan lay in the stern, his hand on the rudder and his mind busy over the piastres he had made.   There was a chance, he thought, of earning a little more on the way home by picking up a passenger or two.   It was early winter and the Nile was still high, so that from his boat he could look out over the banks and his white sail could be seen from far across the green country.   Evening was drawing on and the river, the cultivated land and the distant desert cliffs were beginning to glow with a wonderful radiance.   The white sails, like great birds' wings floated here and there over the gleaming water,

the smoke of evening fires rose from the brown villages among
the palms and, down by the river bank, their dark figures
outlined against the sky, came troops of women and girls to
draw water.   They lowered the big jars, gathered up their
flowing gowns and stepped into the muddy stream ankle deep,
chattering and laughing as they filled their waterpots.   Hassan's boat passed near one group of them and he arose and
called a greeting, which was returned by some with tittering,
but mostly with reproaches for his boldness, while the older
and less comely coyly drew the edge of their garment over
their faces.   The boat swept swiftly round a bend of the river
when suddenly, as Hassan steered it close to the bank, a girl
appeared above, panting with haste and hailed him with the
call to a ferryman ' Take me up, take me up, O boatman.'   He
turned the prow to the bank and looked doubtfully at her
unveiled face.   ' Why does a girl like you want to go sailing ?
It means no good.'   She was young and very pretty and
looked at him with big appealing eyes.   ' No good, no good ;
but they will kill me, take me up, save me.'   Hassan hesitated,
but she sprang into the water towards him and he held out his
arms and pulled her in.   ' I will take the risk,' he muttered.
Then round went the tiller and up stream the boat, quickly, yet
not quickly enough to escape the eyes of the women below,
who had paused in their jar-filling to watch the scene.   ' Aziza
has gone,' they cried ; ' the boatman has taken her.'   ' Will
her people find her now ? ' ' She is shameless, she did well to
flee.   By Allah, the boatman did not need much persuading.'
They chattered on while they helped each other to raise the
heavy jars to their heads, then, steadying them for a moment
with their hands, marched off towards the village.   Along the
paths through the fields were other moving groups, labouring
men, women and children, flocks and herds, all with faces
turned homewards, but presently they met with three or four
stern-faced   men   running   the   opposite   way.   ' Where is
Aziza ? ' they asked.   ' Yonder, yonder,' called the women,
pointing out the distant speck of white sail.   The curses of
the men poured forth.   Said the eldest at length, ' How can we
find her now ?   She will flaunt her shame through all the
country and our house will be disgraced for ever.'   Another
then spoke.   ' The man is a fool who took her.   Can he sail
when the wind drops ?   We have but to take the evening train
and await him where we think fit.   He shall pay dear for his

night's work.' They turned and paced back to the village. It was sunset and the hour of prayer, and after their devotions were duly paid they returned to the discussion of their plans.

" Meanwhile the little boat flew gaily on for an hour or two before the wind. Darkness fell, but lasted briefly, for it was the night of full moon and the sheen had not faded from the river nor the crimson flush from the west, when the eastern sky began to brighten and the moonlight flooded all the land. But the breeze grew lighter and the boat glided more and more slowly on till at last only an occasional puff of wind would catch the sail. They were nearing now a town on the west bank. ' Had we not better,' said Dahshur, ' tie up on the opposite side? It would be quieter.' ' Nay,' returned Hassan ' safety for me is at the town. It is well guarded and there can be no fear from Aziza's people if we moor at the landing-place among all the other boats.' They brought the boat along near a flight of tumbledown steps, fastened it securely, then occupied themselves with preparing supper and a comfortable rest for the night. Lights in the town went out gradually, even the Greek café on the river front subsided into silence and sleep fell upon land and water. But they were still awake in the boat when there came down the stair with tottering steps a very old man, who looked round for a moment at the other boats, then advanced to Hassan's and quavered out, ' Take me up, take me up, O boatman.' ' We take none to-night,' said the lad. The old man turned appealingly to Hassan. ' Wilt thou not take me up? I go but to Nag Hamadi to see my son. I will give thee fifteen piastres.' ' Come in the morning, then,' said Hassan. ' I sail at the dawn.' ' Allah reward thee for it, Allah preserve thee ; yet take me now, thou seest that I am old and there is no place I can go to and come again at the dawn. Let me get on board with thee now : I will disturb no one.' ' So be it, if thou wilt lie quiet in the prow, come and welcome.' ' Allah protect thee, I thank thee ; I go but to bring my bundle which I left at the top of the steps.' He climbed up toilsomely and disappeared behind a wall where three other men were waiting. They drew together when the old man came towards them and listened eagerly as he whispered, ' It is done, I lie in the bow of the boat. Two hours after midnight, if they are all asleep, I will cut the rope and set us adrift and then, ye have your boat, ye know your work.'

" He advanced again to the top of the steps, carrying his bundle of clothes and food, descended and clambered into the boat. Hassan had spread a warm quilt for himself and Aziza in the stern, Dahshur wrapped up his head and curled himself among the sails in the middle while the old passenger fumbled in his parcel till he produced a brown blanket in which he rolled himself and, after a few salutations, silence fell on the little company.

" The night hours passed : the broad river and the land were clear and calm in the brilliant moonlight ; no sound was heard save the distant barking of dogs and the call of the village guards as they passed on their rounds. Of the four who lay in the boat, three were sleeping soundly, when, at two hours after midnight, the old man in the bows turned himself cautiously, drew a long knife from his gown, and cut the rope that tied them to the mooring post. Silently they glided out into the stream and floated down, the water lapped lightly on the sides of the boat, the freshness of a rising breeze met them, but no warning disturbed the slumbers of the ill-fated crew.

" Presently another boat slipped out from the bank, manned by three men and drifted down after the first. The current bore them along steadily and surely towards a sandbank on the opposite side and when Hassan's boat came close by it, the old man stepped out into the shallow water and drew it slowly in. The other boat grounded a few yards higher up.

" Three men from it sprang out and came swiftly towards the sleepers. The old man pointed to the lad Dahshur, now lying with upturned face in the moonlight. ' Let him alone, he had nought to do with it. There in the stern are those whom ye seek.'

" Quick as thought one man leaped on the boat, raised aloft a weighty adze and swung it round on the head of the sleeping Hassan. So sudden was his death-blow that he never awoke, but with one convulsive gesture sank to rest for ever. The girl beside him woke with a start and a cry ; she saw the murdered man and the fierce faces of her kinsmen ; one of them grasped her roughly and bid her go before him to the other boat ; and Aziza knew that her hour had come.

" A few minutes more and the smaller boat was being rapidly rowed down-stream, the plash of its oars dying away in the distance. The lonely boy, Dahshur, just awake and bewildered with grief and terror, sat up and looked at his dead brother, scarcely knowing if this were an evil dream or real. Then he burst into wild sobbing and wailed aloud, ' Alas, my brother ! Alas, my brother. Help.' Louder and louder he raised his voice and in time the sound of his weeping was carried to the guards in the town, and two of them crossed in a boat to see what was amiss. The lad gasped out his tale to them and they were much amazed and pitied him greatly. It was just before dawn and the first summons to prayer was sounding from the minaret of the little mosque when they reached the town again. ' Prayer is better than sleep, Prayer is better than sleep.' But it was not to prayer that the police authorities were roused that morning, but to hear this wild tale of what had happened in the night."

As the story was told to us, there was little concern felt at the very proper punishment of wrongdoing in a family, but some regret was expressed at the inevitable miscarriage of justice that had taken place. For the point was, that the only arrest and conviction made in connexion with the affair was that of Dahshur, who was brought in guilty of the murder of his brother and condemned to fifteen years in the convict prison, there being no evidence against anybody else !

CHAPTER XII

CAIRO TO LUXOR: THE ANTIQUITIES

IT is rather difficult, in describing antiquity sites, to keep a due sense of proportion. Some are so important historically, some have yielded such treasure for literature or archæology, that one is tempted to dilate on them too enthusiastically ; with others, there may be memories of happy days spent there, or of special guidance which illuminated the problems. This is very present to me when I think of the long stretch of over four hundred miles between Cairo and Luxor. Full as it is of interest, how many of the sites are there which would really be impressive to travellers ? I mean to intelligent and educated travellers, not familiar with Egypt and Egyptian archæology. Leaving out Sakkara, which is of the highest importance, is there any other place which should be classed among the very best ? I can only think of Abydos. And Abydos can be seen, with a little effort, either from Luxor, or on the way down from Luxor to Cairo, whereas the places in Middle Egypt are exceedingly hard to get at. From the tourist steamer Beni Hassan and Assiout are visited, but, of Beni Hassan at least, it will be the memory of the great view from the cliff that will remain in our minds rather than the paintings in the tombs.

Still, there is so much to say about all this tract of country, that in a single chapter one can hardly skim the surface. Let us think first of the Pyramid area, which stretches down from Cairo as far as Wasta, about an hour by express train. Giza we have seen and Sakkara we have seen : Dahshur we have often looked at, but not many people have been there. What one wants to remember about Dahshur is that the two

big pyramids are very ancient indeed ; coming in order
between the Step Pyramid which is oldest of all, and the
Giza group. The smaller pyramids of Dahshur are of the
Middle Empire, *circ.* 2000 B.C. ; they are built of brick and
in a ruinous state, but it was in the entrance passage of the
northern of these that the superb Dahshur jewellery was
found.

The next group is at Lisht, where there are two pyramids,
also of the Middle Empire and also much ruined. They were
never very large, but they had magnificent temples, which
have been excavated by the Metropolitan Museum of New
York, but had been thoroughly plundered and quarried away
in antiquity. These pyramids are to be seen from the railway
near the little station of Matania, but only the slowest of
slow trains stop there. Nearing Wasta, there is another and
a particularly interesting one. It is known as the Pyramid
of Medum and is the next stage in development after the
Step Pyramid of Sakkara. It is in steps, too, but the steps
are higher, the slope steeper and the shape square instead of
being slightly oblong, like a mastaba. It was built by Seneferu, the first king of the Fourth Dynasty, but apparently
he was not satisfied with the design, for, in all probability,
he afterwards built the northern of the two big Dahshur
pyramids and was buried there. This Medum pyramid is
very imposing from near at hand and there were splendid
tombs round about it. Every one knows the statues of
Rahotep and Nefert, which are among the finest things in
Cairo. They were found at Medum and it is related that in
the darkness of the tomb their eyes gleamed and flashed so
that the workmen were terrified to come near them.

The railway to the Fayum branches off from Wasta and
crosses a strip of desert, but there is a fair road for motor-
cars from Beni Suef, which follows the ancient route along
a canal bank. The original canal here was a Middle Empire
work, made to regulate the outflow from the Lake, which
at that time covered most of the present area of the Fayum.
Two of the kings made their pyramids in this district : Sesostris
II at Illahun and Amenemhat III at Hawara. The temple

of Amenemhat's pyramid was known to the Greeks as the
Labyrinth and its beauty was much extolled by them. But
perhaps none of the great Egyptian monuments has been so
destroyed past all recognition as this temple. It was built
of very fine white limestone, and many more precious stones
were used in its construction, but now only chips and limestone
dust strew the ground where it stood. Sir Flinders Petrie
has excavated round both these pyramids as well as the
town which Sesostris II built for his workmen. It was only
inhabited while the pyramid was being built, so everything
found there is very exactly dated to his reign and this has
much extended our rather scanty knowledge of the Middle
Empire.

Returning to the Nile Valley, there comes a dull bit of
country between Beni Suef and Minia. Cemeteries there
are on the desert edge, all the way, but no very important
ones. The modern towns are flourishing, and in the cultivation we begin to notice the sugar plantations which are a
feature of Middle Egypt, but otherwise the crops and the
villages are much the same as lower down. For hours the
train runs along the large Ibrahamieh canal, on which the
cultivation mainly depends. Minia is a big, wealthy place,
where anyone who wants to visit the sites that lie between it
and Assiout can find fair accommodation, but these places
are difficult of access. One generally has to stay the night
at Minia and leave it at an unearthly hour in the morning,
getting off at a little station and riding a long way on a very
feeble little donkey. If one has introductions to a local
magistrate or landowner and can borrow a horse, it makes
it much simpler. It is possible to get to Beni Hassan and
back in a day from Minia, either by riding, or by taking train
to Abu Kerkas, ferrying over the river and walking to the
tombs. These lie on the east bank, and are much more easily
seen from a boat ; in fact they are one of the regular stops
for the tourist steamers.

The Beni Hassan tombs have been well known for a long
time and it is scarcely possible to overrate their importance,
but I think they must be a sad disappointment to most people.

They have suffered from long exposure and also from the early copyists, who used some varnish or other medium to bring out the colours, which has had the effect of darkening the surface so much that it is now very difficult to see anything.   It is all there ; the wealth of scenes and the beautiful detail, but I am persuaded that the majority of visitors who go in for half an hour or so out of the brilliant sunlight, see nothing at all, except the big caves in the rock and the view up and down the Nile.

Nearly everything that is known about the daily life of the Middle Empire comes from these tombs.   The great monarchy of the Old Empire had fallen some centuries before ; anarchy succeeded to it, and when a new order slowly evolved, Egypt appears much more like a feudal state than it had been in the earlier age, when the government was much centralized. In the Eleventh and Twelfth Dynasties, there were powerful kings reigning, who are buried in pyramids near the old capital of Memphis—we have seen them at Dahshur and Lisht —but there were also provincial nobles, who lived almost like kings themselves, but owed military service to the Pharaoh. The Beni Hassan tombs belonged to one of these families, and cover several generations.

The scenes are painted on plaster, not carved in relief as at Sakkara, and as the tombs are very large, very high and covered with paintings to the very top, it is evident that much of it would have been difficult to see, even if the paint had been freshly put on.   There are many of the same scenes as at Sakkara, but there are new features about them and many others are seen here for the first time.

A famous group of Asiatics and Bedouin bringing tribute used to be claimed as portraits of the sons of Jacob on their way down to Joseph in Egypt.   There is, of course, no evidence for this whatever, but the dating is probably about right, and the elaborate dresses and the extremely Semitic profiles do gain in interest for us when we reflect that the Children of Israel must have looked very much like that to the Egyptians.   Besides the usual pictures of harvesting, carpentering and all other activities, there is a great deal that

is simply concerned with amusements. Boys wrestling, girls
playing ball games, and as always, much hunting and fishing.
Apparently at this time, it was the custom for a big " shoot "
to enclose part of the desert with a net and to drive the game
into it. Battles too, are there, and one of the oldest repre-
sentations of the siege of a fortress. In the Middle Empire
it is known that frontier forts were built above the Second
Cataract, to keep off the negro tribes that were pressing down
from the Sudan. Another in the Wady Tumilat, near where
the railway from Cairo to Ismailia now runs, was made
against the Bedouin and perhaps this is a picture of how
Chnemhotep, the owner of the tomb, held it for his king.
The inscriptions are not so full as we should like, but there
is a great deal more than there used to be in the older tombs.
Some of the princes tell a good deal about the public events
of their lives and how much they did for their province.

Amenemhat says :

" Not the daughter of a poor man did I wrong ; not a widow
did I oppress ; not a farmer did I beat ; not a herdsman did I
drive off. There was not a foreman of five men from whom I
took his men for the works. There was not a pauper round
me ; there was not a hungry man in my time."

The rest of this long inscription tells of the action he took
during a period of low Niles to avoid famine and of the abundant prosperity which crowned his labours. All of it a pleasing
picture. The rulers of Egypt in the nineteenth century A.D.
could hardly have given the same account of themselves.
Opposite to Beni Hassan the country is wide and the cemeteries
are almost impossible to reach except by camping. There
are eight or nine miles of cultivation to ride over, the Bahr
Yusuf to cross, another bit of fertile land and a strip of low
desert before we reach the western cliffs in which are many
tombs of the Middle Empire, which must once have rivalled
Beni Hassan in beauty, but now are in a terrible state of
devastation.

South of these are the cemeteries belonging to Eshmunein,
once a very large town, and, not very long ago, a lofty mound,

but so much has been carried away by the fellahin to fertilize their fields that it is now little above the level of the rest of the ground.   In this process a good many things have been found, but undoubtedly a great deal more has been irrecoverably lost.

We had a curious glimpse of the survival of ancient beliefs there once, when the "sebakhin" had uncovered a huge granite statue of Merenptah, which is now in Cairo Museum. It made a great sensation in the country, and, while it lay waiting for the necessary tackle to take it to the river, it became a regular pilgrim resort.   Women who wanted to have children brought offerings of fruit and flowers to it, sick people came hoping for a cure, and one man who carried a sick child in his arms, walked three times round the colossal figure, vowing to sacrifice a lamb if his child should be healed.

A more attractive place to visit, lies, like Beni Hassan, on the east bank and near the river. This is Tell el Amarna, and it, in many ways, is unique. All other Egyptian towns are on the cultivation ; this is on the desert ; all others have a long history ; this lasted for one generation. Being on the desert, there was plenty of room and every house was a detached villa, with garden space round about. It was on the low desert, so water was not too far down and many houses had private wells within their enclosures. The capital was moved from Thebes hurriedly and the new town must have been built very quickly. That was easy, for houses and palaces are all of brick; whitewash and paint are soon applied and when we think of the rapid, not to say slap-dash, style of Tell el Amarna decoration, we can quite understand that a very short time would be enough to build the place and that the effect would be very pleasing. A keen wind blows over that bit of open desert, but most of the houses had balconies both to north and south and a great part of the time was spent out of doors even in winter. Being on the desert, the ruins have not been much carried away by the "sebakhin" and it has been possible to work out plans of houses of every description.

A few very beautiful pieces of sculpture have been found

here, others may yet be found, but never many. Such pieces are rare at any time, and for the short bloom of Tell el Amarna the quantity of work on the tomb walls must have occupied the artists completely. The tombs are in the cliffs, about three miles across the low desert. They were full of lovely scenes, but have suffered frightful damage. What remains has been carefully copied by Mr. de Garis Davies, who has recovered many interesting pieces. From these tombs have come one or two versions of the Hymn to the Aten, a splendid religious poem, which in itself suffices to shed a glory over Akhenaten and his city.

The grave of Akhenaten lies far up a lonely wady, so remote, one would think, that it would have been safe from wilful damage. But even here the sculptures have suffered terribly, probably from reprisals by the Amen priesthood after the return to the old worship. Akhenaten's body was not allowed to rest there. It was found about twenty years ago, in a tomb in the Valley of the Tombs of the Kings at Thebes, enclosed in a magnificent coffin, but with no funerary equipment, except four alabaster Canopic jars, each with his portrait on the lid. These are exquisite things ; among the few great gems that have come down to us.

It is not known what happened in regard to his burial, but most likely, when the reaction came—and it came soon and violently—some of the king's old servants and office bearers must have saved the royal body from the destruction that was imminent and conveyed it back to Thebes in secret. No one will ever know how Tell el Amarna ended. The entire episode seems like an impossible romance, but we have the portraits and the hymn to give assurance of its reality.

We come down to everyday modern life again at Assiout, a wealthy place prettily situated. It has a great history behind it, for perhaps no town in the world has gone on so continuously since 3000 B.C.

In the Feudal age of the Middle Empire it belonged to a great family whose tombs are in the hill behind ; in the New Empire it was much devoted to the worship of the Jackal god Anubis. Large cemeteries of mummified dogs and jackals

have been found in the vicinity ; also their funerary stelæ,
with pictures of the dogs on them, sometimes an animal
alone, sometimes surrounded by a litter of puppies.   The
Greeks called Assiout Lycopolis, as this wolf, or jackal worship
was still very prominent in that epoch.   It is a very prettily
situated town and a ramble on the hill behind it is interesting
and enjoyable.   The ancient tombs are much ruined, but
some of the better preserved of the little rock chambers were
taken possession of by anchorites in the early centuries
of Christianity and used as cells.   The walls are painted
with figures of saints and religious scenes, more devotional
than artistic, it is true, but very characteristic of their
period.

Throughout the Middle Ages Assiout remained an important
place ; one reason for this being that it is at the end of a
caravan route from Darfur, by which slaves and other produce
of the Sudan used to be brought into Egypt.   Both Belzoni
and Miss Martineau mention this and shed the same unsavoury
light upon the slave trade and its results.

Belzoni :

" Siout is the capital of Upper Egypt.   There is a constant
commerce kept up by the caravans from Darfur.   Negroes,
feathers, elephant's teeth, and gum, are the principal articles
brought to market.   The viceroy of Upper Egypt is always
the first to select what he pleases from the caravan ; for which
he fixes his own price, and pays what he likes.   The rest is for
merchants, who dare not buy anything till the viceroy has
made his choice.

" This place is celebrated for the making of eunuchs.   As
soon as the operation is performed the boys are buried in the
ground, all but the head and shoulders ; and many, who are
not of strong constitution, die with the excruciating pain.   It
is calculated, that the operation during its performance or
afterwards, proves fatal to two out of three.

" Besides the usual produce of the country, wheat, beans,
flax, and seeds, a great number of wax candles are made ; and
it is from hence Cairo is supplied with this article.   Ibrahim
Bashaw has latterly been the terror of the people.   When an
unfortunate culprit was brought before him, after some few

11

questions, he sent him to the Cady to be judged. This was
the signal for taking him to a particular cannon, to the mouth
of which he was tied ; and it was then fired off, loaded with a
ball, so that the body was scattered about in pieces at a considerable distance. In the case of two Arabs, who had killed
a soldier, not without provocation, this Bashaw had them fastened to a pole, like two rabbits on a spit, and roasted alive at
a slow fire : yet this man is now heir to the government of
Egypt on the death of Mahomet Ali."

In modern times Assiout has become most progressive.
It owes a great deal to the American Mission schools, which
have had immense influence on the community, especially
on the Copts, who form the most important part of the population and some of whom are among the richest men in Egypt.
The wealth of all this part has increased enormously since the
making of the Assuan dam. Assiout possesses a subsidiary
Barrage, which regulates the irrigation of Middle Egypt and
acts both as a reservoir and as a distributor. It feeds the
Ibtrahimia canal, which requires a supply all the year round,
and it also holds up the level of the water in flood time sufficiently to fill the line of basins on the edge of the desert.

Above Assiout I always feel that the country and the people
are pleasanter, at least the Upper Egypt fellahin are the class
with whom I get on best and feel most at home. The cultivated strip is narrower and usually more attractive. Above
Assiout, as below, there is a continuous line of cemeteries on
the western desert, which it would only be wearisome to note
in any detail. But there are great Christian monuments at
Sohag, which must not be passed over. The White and Red
Monasteries are among the most ancient buildings of Christendom and stand, fortress like, on the desert edge, as if wave
after wave of plundering Bedouin and fanatic Muslim foes has
dashed against them and left them unimpaired.

The White Monastery is supposed to have been founded
by St. Helena, and undoubtedly does date from a very early
period, probably fourth century. It has a certain look about
it as of an ancient Egyptian temple, as it is finished off at
the top with a fine cornice, and the interior columns have

been taken from pagan temples. Most of the building is occupied by the magnificent church, but there is a corridor running the whole length of the church, where the monks live. The interior was once very richly decorated, but it was burned in the beginning of the nineteenth century by the retreating Mamelukes, and little trace remains of its former beauty. It is larger than the Red Monastery and better worth seeing, but this excursion will only attract people who are interested in ancient Christian architecture, for the place in itself is gloomy enough.

Opposite to Sohag is Ekhmim, a fair-sized town with a large Christian population. It is still noted for its weaving and some of the designs which linger on are quite interesting. Once it was an immense place, but nothing could be more dismal than the vast surrounding mound now is, for the soil has been carried off by the sebakhin and robbers have ravaged it for the antiquities.

On towards Girga the desert cliffs stand out grandly on the east side. Somewhere near here was the site of Thinis, the capital of the early kings, Menes and his successors, before they moved down to Memphis. On the western desert lies Abydos, where they are buried. The nearest station to it is Baliana, but a good many miles of rather dull road lie between the railway and the temple. It is a good, flat road, easy going for donkeys, and there is even a carriage to be got at the station, a real old-fashioned cab, mostly tied together by string, but it is believed to convey travellers safely.

But, by whatever means of transport, the goal to be reached is well worth the effort. Abydos was the holiest place in Egypt, sanctified by the graves of the ancient kings that lie out on the desert, near the gorge where their father Ra sinks to rest in the western mountain, sanctified even more by the legend that there the god Osiris, who died and rose again, lay buried after his brother slew him. It is hardly possible to disentangle the primitive part of this tale from the mass of later mythology that gathered round it, but there is little doubt that all the higher side of Egyptian religion was bound up with the Abydos worship and that the mysteries celebrated there did set forth the resurrection from the dead and the judgments in the world to come.

The temple was built by Seti Ist and is most beautiful. It was dedicated to Osiris, but to all the great gods of Egypt there are chapels, perhaps emphasizing thus the underlying unity of the Divine principle. Not only are the gods adored, but in one corridor is a fine relief, which shows Seti and his son Rameses making offerings to the deified kings their predecessors, whose names are written up in long rows of cartouches.

Behind and below the Seti temple is an older one at a lower level. This is a very impressive sight, for it is built of gigantic granite blocks, like the granite temple at Giza and is probably of the same date. But it is just possible that it may be a solitary remaining great work of the Middle Empire when the Osiris cult became very general. There is nothing to tell us. The only inscription on it is by Merenptah, who most certainly never built it. Behind this again, are other buildings which do date from his time, but have only been partially excavated. The accumulation of sand would be very expensive to move, but it is to be hoped that at some future time this may be undertaken and perhaps some light thrown on the mysterious ritual that was conducted there.

Osiris was worshipped all over Egypt and at all times, but the devotion to him increased as ages went by, and, while the everyday religion seems to have sunk more and more into the gross superstition of animal worship, the Osiris cult undoubtedly grew purer and loftier as the centuries and millenniums passed. Here, at his central shrine, some feeling of the holiness of the place descends upon us out of the distant past. It was a place of pilgrimage for the living and the dead. To be buried in the Abydos cemetery, or even to send a stela there as a representative, acquired merit for the deceased, while crowds from every part of Egypt flocked there for the celebration of the Mysteries.

Back to the train, and the railway brings us down from the higher life to the material one. And there is nothing at Baliana, or for some way onwards, to arouse us again.

A railway starts from the Oasis Junction and runs westwards to Khargeh, a place I much regret never having seen. It is a large oasis, but was apparently more fertile in ancient times than nowadays.   There is a very complete temple there, built by the Persian kings and an extensive Christian cemetery, with interesting painted tombs.   Khargeh was rather favoured by the Alexandrian patriarchs as a place of banishment for heretics and a good deal is known about it from the writings of some of the early fathers, but its history since then has been obscure.

Soon after passing the Oasis Junction the railway crosses the Nile at Nag Hamadi, where there is a large sugar factory, but nothing else to mention.   Once across, the cultivation is narrow and there are pleasant views of desert cliffs on both sides.   We begin to see the dôm palms which are a feature of the Thebaid.   The only important place north of Luxor is Keneh, which is a most thriving little town, the seat of a Mudirièh and the station from which to visit the temple of Dendera.   Dendera is well worth seeing as being a Ptolemaic temple in complete preservation.   It is very like Edfu in plan ; not so large and not so fine, but still a very magnificent place.

From Keneh eastwards is the road over to the Red Sea, which has been described in our chapter on Desert Travel. In old times the road may have started at Kift or Quft, the next station, and some of the earliest invaders who came into the Nile Valley probably settled there and gave it the name of Coptos, by which the Christian inhabitants of the country are still called, and from which comes the Greek " Ægyptos " and the modern " Egypt."

A little farther, and we see the pylons of Karnak, the palm groves of Luxor and, on the western bank, the high red cliffs above the City of the Dead.

CHAPTER XIII

LUXOR: THE EAST BANK

MORE than four hundred miles to the south of Cairo, and the Nile is still as wide as ever and flowing as peacefully through its narrow belt of green between the great deserts to east and west. But, monotonous and unchanging as it seems, the landscape up here is different, and so is the climate. For three or four months at Luxor and Assuan, the weather is as near perfection as it is granted to anything on this planet to be ; for three or four more, the heat is bearable, as there come days or even weeks of good wind, when the mornings are fresh and the evenings cool. But as to the rest of the year——! Summer can be tolerable, even enjoyable, in Cairo under good conditions, but for Europeans in Upper Egypt, the summer months must just be endured and lived through as best they may be, with little to mitigate the awful heat.

In winter, the green is more vivid than in the north, the desert more rosy, the river more mirror-like. One gorgeous day follows another, from brilliant dawn till flaming sunset ; stillness and peace steal over us, and bring forgetfulness and dreamy calm. And, over and above the slumbrous beauty of the land, we live among some of the grandest ruins of antiquity, while the noblest burying-place in all the world lies folded away among the red cliffs across the Nile.

Thebes is not old as Memphis is old, but it is older than anything else. When Homer wrote of " hundred gated Thebes," it was already long past its best. All of its greatest buildings had been standing for centuries and so much still stands that we get more into the Past here in southern Egypt than anywhere else in the country. There is not much to remind us of the long time that has intervened.

Once there was mighty Thebes, with kings and priests and people, with palaces, temples and pylons ; now there is the poor little modern town, but the two thousand years and more that separate them are almost blank. Gradually, as the old city fell into ruin, its débris accumulated round and over the temple and houses were built upon the rubbish until it grew into high mounds. At one time a great part of the population squatted upon the temple roof, and only the pylon and the tops of the columns rose from among the rambling brick dwellings. But this preserved the place, and as it is now cleared, the splendid architecture is seen from end to end.

It is not easy to form an idea of what the ancient town looked like, nor even how large it was, nor where the royal palace may have been. Perhaps the strongest impression we should have, if we could put ourselves back into the past, is of vivid colour. The houses were of mud brick, as Egyptian houses always have been, but they were painted white or yellow with gay decoration, and there were many villas standing by themselves in formal gardens, with large shady trees and square pools of water. Near the river bank rose the temple, covered with brilliant painting, with four huge flags waving from its lofty pylon. The river was crowded with shipping, and the dahabiehs of the wealthy people had gorgeous cabins on the deck, covered with hangings of woven tapestry. The funeral barges that crossed to the west were also as bright as they could be made, with decorated coffins, lying under a canopy of blue and red. The mourners, though robed in sober white and grey, chanted and tore their hair and filled the boats that followed in procession with their wailing. Add to all this the craft that came and went from the Sudan and from Lower Egypt, which filled Luxor in its palmy days with gold and spices, leopard skins, ivory and slaves, and if we picture the noise and tumult of landing and embarking all these, we feel that no description could exaggerate the liveliness or the kaleidoscopic brilliancy of the quays.

The religious ceremonies and processions, too, must have been singularly gay and bright. Within the temple it was much darker than out of doors, but in that latitude even a small window lets in a surprising amount of light, and the ritual performed by large companies of priests and acolytes among the columns and corridors of that most beautiful of temples was evidently very impressive. It is not known how much part was taken by the general public in the ceremonies within the temple, but festivals were frequent in which everybody joined, and apparently the whole town followed in procession when the sacred barque of Amen was carried from Luxor to Karnak along the avenue of sphinxes which leads from the one temple to the other.

The temple walls, both at Luxor and Karnak, are covered with pictures of this procession, and tradition and legends about it have lingered until the present day. I once had the luck to be at Keneh on the fifteenth day before the beginning of Ramadan, when the whole place was holding a festival and a procession was going on. The centre point of the procession was a boat, a large wooden boat, which was being dragged along the streets on rollers, accompanied by a joyous crowd, who no doubt believed that they were celebrating the " festa " of a Mohammedan saint.

The late M. Legrain, in the course of his long years' residence at Karnak, heard many tales of the glamour that still hangs round the temples, especially of the golden boat that may at times be seen to float upon the waters of the Sacred Lake.

Karnak has had a different history from Luxor, as it lay far out of the modern town and never was built over. But it has suffered more than Luxor, for it is said to have been in great part destroyed by one of the severe earthquakes which occasionally have visited Egypt. Even without that catastrophe, the total neglect of more than two thousand years would be enough to explain a very great deal of damage. It was the task of M. Legrain, who spent twenty-eight years at Karnak, to set up again the forest of columns which compose the Hypostyle Hall and to carry out a great amount of restoration in the rest of the temple.

PLATE IX

KARNAK FROM THE SACRED LAKE

So the visitor of to-day sees a Karnak much more like what it originally was than any of the early travellers did. The Temple has been well planned and its history worked out, so that it is possible for those who take sufficient trouble, to understand a great deal about it. It is well worth while for every one to try to get hold of its main divisions, especially the limits of the older temple, which was built and completed in the Eighteenth Dynasty, and the immense additions which were made to it in the Nineteenth. The one was before Tell el Amarna ; the other after it, when Amen of Thebes had come back to his own and to greater glory than he had ever had before. Besides these two principal parts of the temple, there were many later additions and many subsidiary temples and pylons built round it at every period down to the Romans. It is a difficult and confusing place ; even after all we can read about it and see of it in repeated visits, we are left with a feeling of amazement at its vastness rather than whole-hearted admiration of its beauty. It is very, very fascinating to spend time there and to explore, day by day, more of the halls and temples and gradually to find the solemnity of the place grow on us as we begin to understand it, till we come to realize what the central shrine of such a temple meant, and we enter it with a kind of awe and see the stone pedestal inside, where the sacred Barque rested, close guarded by massive doors.

Into this tabernacle at some festivals, the King entered, alone, having performed the ceremonies of purification and the rites of early morning. He ascended the steps, he unlocked the door at the eastern end of the shrine and saw his father Amen Ra, rising to shed his beams over the land.

This shrine was destroyed long ago, not by earthquake, but by enemies. The deed seems to have been done by the last Persian conquerors of Egypt, who were driven out by Alexander the Great. Alexander was himself received among the gods of the country and acknowledged as the bodily son of Amen Ra, but he was in too great haste to go on with his world conquest to go up to Thebes to visit the chief sanctuary of his father the god ; indeed, probably the shrine was at that time in so ruinous a state that no ceremony could have been carried out in it.   But it is likely that he gave the order for its restoration, for it was one of the earliest works taken in hand by his successor in Egypt, Ptolemy Soter, who, in fact, did it in the name of Philip Arridæus, the regent over the Empire during the lifetime of Alexander's posthumous son. It was only after the boy emperor died and Philip Arridæus was murdered that Ptolemy assumed the titles of King of Egypt.

The reliefs in this granite shrine are almost certainly reproductions of the originals and give an interesting description of the Barque being lifted from its pedestal and carried in procession round the temple.   Another part of Karnak which is very attractive in a different way is the Festival Hall of Thothmes III, built for one of his Jubilees and including several rooms or open courts, decorated with reliefs representing the birds, animals and flowers that Thothmes had brought back from one of his many campaigns in Palestine. It would seem that he planted a garden of these in Karnak and tried to grow the imported plants, but it is very difficult to identify them, as the colour has disappeared and the treatment is quite conventional, but it is an entertaining place, and a sort of relief after the colossal figures and gloomy, mysterious temples through which we have passed.

From the top of the pylon there is a great view of the river and the ruins, but the most picturesque sight of them is from the Sacred Lake (Plate IX).   This admirable view of the Hypostyle Hall, the two standing obelisks, part of the Eighteenth Dynasty temple and some of the subsidiary buildings is as comprehensive as can be taken in from any one point.

Anyone who is a tolerable walker will find a pleasant route to Karnak along the river bank.   Near the house of the Inspector of Antiquities, is a little path close to the Nile, which, unless it has been interfered with by recent building, makes a delightfully quiet walk down to the river front of Karnak.   And, coming back to Luxor, one may go through the Temple of Mut, with its horseshoe-shaped lake and the ring of cat-headed goddesses sitting round it, and out by a side gate and on through the fields towards the town.

The Temple of Luxor is a finer thing architecturally, and much easier to understand than Karnak (Plate X). Here we have the same two great epochs, the Eighteenth Dynasty and the Nineteenth, before and after Tell el Amarna, but only those two, and actually, here, the intervening time was very short, so there is a unity of scheme. Plate X shows the pillared courtyard built by Amenhotep III. It was begun by him, just the very reign before the Tell el Amarna revolution, and it looks as if he must have been desperately anxious to justify his title as the son of Amen, for not only did he build this great temple to the honour of the god, but he added to it a hall where the decoration is entirely devoted to his claim to divinity. His mother, Mutemua, was a foreign princess. It was the first time that a foreigner had mingled with the blood royal of Egypt and there may well have been those among the Amen priesthood who considered that this excluded the divine descent, which carried the right to wear the crown of Egypt. Amenhotep did what his predecessor Hatshepsut had done on her funerary temple at Der el Bahri. She was a woman and had to prove a special title to enable her to do anything so unheard of as to reign in her own right, so the pictures there tell the story of how Amen Ra visited the beautiful Queen Ahmes and made her the mother of Hatshepsut, who was reared by all the gods, at his express behest, as his divine daughter. Amenhotep adapts the tale to his own ends and declares that Amen Ra beheld and loved Mutemua and that she bore to him a son, the living image of his father, who should reign over Egypt. One longs to know what really happened afterwards, whether the Priesthood ever genuinely accepted Amenhotep or whether, all through his brilliant reign, some disaffection existed, which found its outlet when he died and left the kingdom to his boy son, Amenhotep the Fourth, but all the power, apparently, to his wife, the great queen Tyi. At all events, it was very soon after Amenhotep died that his widow and his son broke away from Amen Ra, and all the other deities of Egypt, and proclaimed the unity of God as manifested in the power of the Solar Disc. Doubtless the priesthood had been making extrav-

agant demands and had got the town and district of Thebes
entirely into their hands, since the emancipation from them
involved the transference of the capital to a distant part of
Egypt.

After the short-lived gleam that was Tell el Amarna, and
with the revival of the Amen worship, Horemheb planned
out the Hypostyle Hall in Karnak, which was continued by
Sety and completed by Rameses II, who also built the pylon
and forecourt of the Luxor temple, set up two obelisks and
finished the colonnade.   One of these obelisks is now in the
Place de la Concorde in Paris.   All this is in the best style of
early Nineteenth Dynasty architecture and the statues in the
forecourt are of great beauty.   Rameses is seen with the best
beloved of his many wives, Queen Nefertari, whose graceful
figure scarcely comes up to his colossal knees.   Some of these
statues were visible many years ago, and the upper part of
Amenhotep's columns was above ground, but the impression
of the whole was much spoiled, Miss Martineau says, and
other travellers say, by the intrusion of mud huts along the
entire extent of the temple roof (Plate XI).   It was in one
of these mud houses that another English lady lived some
twenty years later, who looked on Egypt with different eyes.
Lady Duff Gordon had very little interest in the antiquities ;
none, in fact, apart from their picturesqueness, but she spent
the last years of her life in making friends with her Egyptian
neighbours and she left a wonderful memory behind her.
She went to Egypt for her health and took a dahabieh up
the Nile for the winter of 1862–3, but found that it would
suit her better and at the same time be more economical to
take a house and settle down in Upper Egypt.   She obtained
the use of a rambling old building on the roof of the Luxor
temple, which had been lived in by Salt and Belzoni, had
subsequently become the property of the French Government
and was known as the Maison Française.   Here she passed
the greater part of three years, leaving it only when the
heat grew unbearable and returning early in the winter.   She
loved it, and loved the south-country people.   She learned
a great deal of the language, and the descriptions of their

PLATE X

LUXOR TEMPLE

customs which her letters contain are graphic and accurate.
There is no doubt that she understood and sympathized with
the habits and mentality of the Upper Egypt fellahin, both
men and women, as no one else has ever done, and was much
beloved by them.   I do not think that this is surprising.   It
would be strange if a beautiful, gifted and very warm-hearted
woman, who was full of kindness and compassion for suffering
and oppression, did not call out affection in return.   Certainly
the country people in Upper Egypt, who are very appreciative
of good manners, very susceptible to kindness, especially in
the form of help and relief in pain and sickness, were sure to
respond in overflowing measure.   I am entirely of Lady Duff
Gordon's mind in preferring the upper-country people to the
peasants of Middle and Northern Egypt, but I think that
almost anywhere, if one settled among the people and shared
in their lives, even nowadays, when they are much better
off, there would be a great return of good will and some
affection.   But the price is too heavy for most of us.   When
we have kept house in Egypt for long years and know the
difference it has made to the health of the household to
boil the milk and the water, and to see after the state of the
saucepans and the nature of the cooking fat, it strikes horror
into our hearts to read what she did daily, as a matter of
course, in the way of eating and drinking.   That may seem
a small matter, and indeed it could be got over by taking
a little trouble.   But such things do not really bridge the
gulf.   Without her intense gift of sympathy, her power of
giving herself to the people around her, the differences between
East and West are apt to widen instead of diminish with
increasing contact.   The points of view are too opposed, the
subjects in common are too few, the demand for companionship is too strong for it to be possible for a genuine intimacy
to arise even with every good will on both sides.   Let us be
thankful that some, like Lane and Lady Duff Gordon, have
been able to cross the gulf and to tell us something about the
other side.

Apart from her very sympathetic insight into the life and
religion of the people of Luxor, Lady Duff Gordon's letters

are extremely interesting historically. The years she spent
in Egypt, from 1862 to 1867, were the early years of Ismail
Pasha, and, even then, the misery and destitution of the
peasants were appalling, though no doubt there was worse
to follow. She and other writers say that everything was
done to give Cairo the appearance of a flourishing capital,
but that in the country the oppression was terrible.

" Jan. 11th, 1865. The whole place is in desolation, the
men are being beaten, one because his camel is not good
enough, another because its saddle is old and shabby, and the
rest because they have not enough money to pay the winter
food and the wages of one man to convey four camels, to be
paid for the use of the Government beforehand " [these camels
were being called up as a levy to be sent to the Sudan, of course
with no compensation to the owners, who would never see
them again]. " The courbash has been going on my neighbours' backs and feet all the morning. It is a new sensation,
too, when a friend turns up his sleeve and shows the marks of
the wooden handcuffs and the gall of the chain on his throat.
The system of wholesale extortion and spoliation has reached
a point beyond which it would be difficult to go. I grieve for
Abdallah el Habbashee and men of high position like him
sent to die by disease—or murder—in Fazoglou " [the convict
settlement in the Sudan] " but I grieve still more over the daily
anguish of the poor fellahin, who are forced to take the bread
from the mouths of their starving families and to eat it while
toiling for the private profit of one man."

Her letters are full of such tales, which indeed show what
the condition of Egypt was when things were a little worse
than normal. But the *corvée* and the courbash and the old
land tenure *were* normal until the English occupation, and the
picture Belzoni gives, long before, of the lives of the Egyptian
peasants, though not nearly so sympathetic, is not so very
different.

They have been accustomed to oppression for so long that
perhaps it is only when the oppression is carried to excess
that it is much resented. Though individually they can express their opinions with much force and aptness, they are

inarticulate as a class, and one fears that with the passing of the
English occupation they may be condemned once more to
suffer in silence.

Another feature of Egyptian life that Lady Duff Gordon
saw has gone, we may hope, for ever, namely, the slave
trade. In Ismail's time, the authorities knew perfectly well
that as a civilized power they must not allow any such thing
in Egypt, and travellers were told of the great improvements
that had come about and all that had been done to secure its
suppression. But Lady Duff Gordon lived at Luxor, in the
midst of it, and gives a very different story. More than one
little Nubian waif that had been stranded without a master
or a home was adopted by her, but her general testimony as
to the mildness of Egyptian treatment of slaves is confirmed
by all who knew the country. Once the poor creatures had
been torn away from their homes in Africa and sold to Egyptian masters, they became more or less members of the family,
especially in Upper Egypt where the life was simpler than in
Cairo. Moreover, Mohammedan law protects slave women
who have borne children to their owners ; they cannot be
separated from their children and can even, under some
circumstances, obtain their freedom and marry. But any
society where slavery rules is of necessity cruel. Her descriptions of her friends and their households, of the visits
she paid and received, their strange life stories and their long
discussions on morals and religion, are most interesting and
most delightfully told. She was so popular in Luxor that
she was repeatedly invited into the mosque of Abu'l Heggag
(*vide* Plate XI) to prayers and festivals.

Here is one of her experiences that surely must be unique
for any European.

"I am better and have hardly any cough. The people
here think it is owing to the intercession of Abu'l Heggag, who
specially protects me. I was obliged to be wrapped in the
green silk cover of his tomb when it was taken off to be carried
in procession, partly for my health and general welfare, and as
a sort of adoption into the family. I made a feeble resistance
on the score of being a Nusranee, but was told ' Never fear

does not God know thee and the Sheikh also ?   No evil will come to thee on that account, but good.' "

The mosque of Abu'l Heggag is the last remaining of the brick buildings which used to cover the Temple roof, and many proposals have been made to have the mosque removed and complete the clearance of the temple.   But Abu'l Heggag is a great saint and local feeling is strongly against his being disturbed.   Besides, the little mosque and its minaret sit very picturesquely against the pylon and above the columns and statues of the forecourt, and my sympathies are entirely with those who desire to leave it alone.   Is not Abu'l Heggag also a monument ?

PLATE XI

PYLON AND NORTH END OF LUXOR TEMPLE PREVIOUS TO EXCAVATION

CHAPTER XIV

LUXOR: THE WEST BANK

DOWN at Memphis the royal graves dominate the landscape, but at Thebes the landscape is grander than the mightiest kings could rival, so, in the burying-place of the Theban kings no outward show is made. The valley which leads to the royal tombs is wild and barren at the lower end, but with every turn and winding the cliffs close in upon it and grow higher and steeper, till it opens out in an amphitheatre of precipices (Plate XII). Below these towering red rocks, there are, here and there, small black holes, the tops of stairways that descend into the mountain side. Down these rock-hewn stairs are the corridors and galleries, the store-rooms and burial chambers of the royal tombs. All of it was for the dead king alone : for his use were the sculptures that covered the walls and the furniture that was stored in the rooms. There he was to lie in lonely state, in his massive granite coffin, while his spirit roamed about the tomb, read the magic words, partook of the food and drink, anointed himself with oil and perfumes, lay on the couch at ease, or went hunting in his chariot through the fields of the blessed.

When the stately funeral was over, the door was closed and the stairway filled up with rubble, so that in old times there was not even the little mark on the mountain side to show that a grave was there. As at Giza and Sakkara, we saw that the king was buried and locked up securely in his pyramid so, exactly in the same way, he is here closed up in the recesses of the rock. But we know that every Egyptian tomb had two essential parts, the burial vault and the chapel, or temple

for the memorial services. At Giza and Sakkara temples were
built on the east side of the pyramids for the worshippers of
the dead king, but what happened when the kings were buried
in a lonely and remote place like this ? They must have had
temples too. They had, and very splendid ones, but not in
the Valley. All the desert edge, looking to Luxor, from the
Gurneh temple on the north to Medinet Habu, is one long row
of them. The Gurneh temple was Seti's ; Der el Bahri was
Hatshepsut's, the Ramesseum was Rameses IInd's and
Medinet Habu was the palace as well as the funerary temple
of Rameses III. Between these huge ruins are the foundations of many more, for this was near the town and the cultivated land, easy of access for priests and people ; while,
for the dead kings, the prayers and offerings were just as efficacious as if the two parts of the tomb had been close together
and there was much less risk of disturbance to the graves
away in the well-guarded valley on the other side of the
cliffs.

So, when we go into the Tombs of the Kings, it is like going
into a pyramid : it is the actual burial place and the decoration is just what we should expect to find. There is no
biography or glorification of the dead king, no scenes of
feasting or industry or joyous life. That is all in the temple.
Here we see what it behoved him to know after he had passed
out of this world and gone to make one of the company of
the gods. He had to know how to avail himself of the equipment provided for him here and in the temple, but, most important of all, he had to know how to overcome the dangers
that awaited him. There were troubles and trials to pass
through before he was fully received into glory ; monsters
lay in wait for him ; every hour of the night had its lurking
terror, and he would have been badly off without the magic
texts that cover the walls and provide for every emergency.

This mythology is not very well understood yet. It seems
grotesque and fantastic, but really it has been approached
from the wrong end. It is nearly hopeless to make a reason-
able translation of these religious texts without long preliminary study of the inscriptions in the Sakkara pyramids and on

PLATE XII

ROAD TO VALLEY OF THE TOMBS OF THE KINGS

coffins of the Middle Empire, where the myths are to be found in an earlier form.

The existence of these tombs of the Bibân el Muluk has always been known, though for very long periods they can hardly have been visited. About sixty are now known and numbered, but not all of these are tombs of kings and many of them are quite without decoration. Some belonged to members of the royal family, such as that of Yuaa and Thuaa, the parents of Queen Tyi, and of Maherpra, perhaps a son of Thothmes III by a negro mother. So it is quite possible that there may still be a tomb or two that have escaped notice till the present day, but there is hardly likely to be another royal grave.

When Belzoni was there in 1817, he saw about ten royal tombs and five or six more of a second order and he thought there were no more to be discovered. His famous find was the tomb of Seti Ist, which is the finest of all. His account of this, and of the removal of the alabaster sarcophagus is very vivid and graphic :

" On the 16th (October, 1817) I recommenced my excavations in the valley of Beban el Malook, and pointed out the fortunate spot, which has paid me for all the trouble I took in my researches. I may call this a fortunate day, one of the best perhaps of my life ; I do not mean to say, that fortune has made me rich, for I do not consider all rich men fortunate, but she has given me that satisfaction, that extreme pleasure, which wealth cannot purchase ; the pleasure of discovering what has long been sought in vain, and of presenting the world with a new and perfect monument of Egyptian antiquity, which can be recorded as superior to any other in point of grandeur, style and preservation, appearing as if just finished on the day we entered it ; and what I found in it will shew its great superiority to all others."

He then describes the excavation, the discovery of the stairway, the entrance and his delight and amazement at the size and splendour of the tomb and the beautiful condition of the decoration, all the way down the sloping corridors and galleries and through the chambers to the great burial hall.

" But the description of what we found in the centre of the saloon, and which I have reserved till this place, merits the most particular attention, not having its equal in the world, and being such as we had no idea could exist. It is a sarcophagus of the finest oriental alabaster, nine feet five inches long, and three feet seven inches wide. Its thickness is only two inches : and it is transparent, when a light is placed in the inside of it. It is minutely sculptured within and without with several hundred figures, which do not exceed two inches in height, and represent, as I suppose, the whole of the funeral procession and ceremonies relating to the deceased, united with several emblems, etc. I cannot give an adequate idea of this beautiful and invaluable piece of antiquity, and can only say that nothing has been brought into Europe from Egypt that can be compared with it. The cover was not there : it had been taken out and broken into several pieces, which we found in digging before the first entrance."

Belzoni's description of the whole tomb is very interesting and curious to read nowadays, as, with much that is accurate and well observed, large theories are built upon what seemed good evidence at the time, but afterwards turned out to be totally misleading. It must be remembered that in 1817, hieroglyphs had not yet been deciphered. Champollion and Young were both on the track, but had not come to certainty. Young believed that in " Belzoni's " tomb, he found the cartouches of Necho and Psammetichus, but that only shows that, though he had guessed correctly that the cartouches contained royal names, he had not yet found the alphabetical equivalents of any of the signs. For the tomb is the tomb of Seti, the great king who built the Abydos temple and designed the Hypostyle Hall of Karnak ; one of the most devout worshippers of Amen Ra and one of the noblest characters of Egyptian history, so far as we can discern him through the dimness of the ages.

His mummy lies in Cairo Museum. Belzoni did not find it in the alabaster coffin, for, long before, it had been removed by pious hands, rewrapped and reburied, for safety from plunderers, in a deep pit near Der el Bahri, along with many other of the old kings. The sarcophagus itself had a strange history. Magnificent as it is, Belzoni had great difficulty in getting it sold. He hoped that it would go to the British Museum, but, whether for lack of money to pay the price, or for some other reason, the Trustees did not buy it and, after a good deal of bargaining with different Museums and collectors, it was eventually acquired by Sir John Soane and is now in the little Museum in Lincoln's Inn Fields, which he bequeathed to the nation. A strange environment for it. Most of the Soane collection consists of eighteenth-century furniture, Hogarth prints and such other homely English things. The sarcophagus could only look as it was meant to look, if it could be replaced again among the gods and demons and magic texts, a hundred metres below the red cliffs of the Bibân el Muluk.

Seti's is undoubtedly the finest tomb in the Valley. It is well to see it and one other only, and that other should be the tomb of Amenhotep II, where the mummy, the only one that was found in place, still lies in its quartzite sarcophagus. The small tomb of Tutankhamen, as I write, early in 1925, is still unfinished, but it is practically certain that in it, too, the mummy has been undisturbed, and it will be desirable, if possible, to leave it where it is, but there are difficulties about such an arrangement, into which I need not enter. It can never, in any case, be a suitable tomb for visitors to see, as it has little decoration on the walls, the space is cramped and small and the rooms are on several different levels.

If two or three visits can be made to the Valley, it is possible, of course, to get to know the tombs in detail. My next choice would be that of Merenptah, because of the splendid granite sarcophagus with his portrait carved on its lid ; after that, when it again becomes accessible, the tomb of Thothmes III, where there is no electric light, owing to its remote position, but the difficulty of getting up to the top of the Valley where it is situated and then down into the tomb, increases our astonishment at the splendid oval funeral chamber which has been hollowed out within.

Most of us feel the need of quietness in the Valley, above all other places, and often it is very difficult to get it. If one goes with a large party and must stick to them, it is hopeless, but more independent travellers can do better. I would give earnest counsel to make a day of the royal tombs and not to go back for lunch, either to Luxor, or over the hill to the rest house at Der el Bahri. People will probably remonstrate and think us mad to stay on after the electric light is taken off at one o'clock, but by that time we have seen the tombs and we want to see the Valley. When the carriages have all clattered down the road and the last of the donkeys has jingled up the slope to Der el Bahri, let us seek out a place under the shadow of a great rock and settle down for an hour or two of peace among the solemn cliffs. There is shade at midday and in the early afternoon at the head of the Valley.

After we have rested and filled our souls with the great scene around, there is a choice of ways by which to return. Down the Valley is the dullest ; over the cliff to Der el Bahri is fine and lets us have a beautiful view from the top, but there is better to be done. There are few good walks in Egypt, but there are some, and perhaps the best of them is the path from the Bibân el Muluk to Der el Medineh. It is quite easy for tolerably good walkers, starting from the valley to the right of the path to Der el Bahri and going upwards above the tomb of Thothmes III.

At the top of the pass are the remains of the shelters where the sentinels of old used to be posted to guard the royal cemetery. From this point onwards the view is glorious. All the line of temples lies below us, Seti's the farthest south, in a clump of palms, Der el Bahri, lying right under the precipice, the Ramesseum, and the big bulk of Medinet Habu to the north. On the desert, in a valley to the right of Medinet Habu are the Tombs of the Queens. On the low desert over the hill of the Sheikh Abd el Gurneh and in the surrounding cliffs, is the cemetery of Thebes, of the nobles and the commonalty.

Beyond Medinet Habu, lines on the desert surface show us the palace of Amenhotep III and the big oblong, just on the edge of the cultivated land, enclosed by high mounds, was once a lake, where he took his pleasure boating. Across the

Nile are the temples of Luxor and Karnak and the green country, with three distant peaks closing the prospect.

It is too obvious, perhaps, to say that the more often we can cross to the West Bank the better we shall like it. There is more to see than anywhere else in Egypt and the beauty of the surroundings is so remarkable that every day we spend among them leaves a memory that does not fade in after years.

So much has been written about the temples that it would be out of place to enter into a description here. Only in reference to Der el Bahri, where much clearance has been done lately by Mr. Winlock on behalf of the Metropolitan Museum of New York, it will not be amiss to add a few words to explain how much more there is to see than there was some years ago.

The great temple of Hatshepsut was excavated in the eighteen nineties by the Egypt Exploration Fund, and a few years later their work was continued on the smaller and older temple close by. This proved to be of great interest. It was the funerary temple of a King Mentuhotep, of the Eleventh Dynasty. At that time, Egypt was just beginning to emerge from the period of anarchy which followed the Old Empire, and it was this Theban family who first regained command over the country.

The old custom of burying the kings in pyramids still continued, but Mentuhotep made a new departure. His actual grave was hollowed out of the cliff, but he built his temple at the entrance to it and in the middle of the pillared court, he placed his pyramid. The temple is in a terribly damaged state, but the plan is clear and the fragments of relief found there are fine and very characteristic. Behind the pillared court are five tomb shafts, belonging to the ladies of his hareem. Two beautiful coffins of white limestone were found in these shafts and are now in the Cairo Museum. There are extremely interesting scenes on both of these, and it is not too much to say that the execution is exquisite. One rather charming touch is that each of the ladies claims to be the " only royal favourite."

But we must use careful observation here to get back into the past and imagine what it used to be.

A sloping ramp led up from the desert to the platform on which the temple stands, and, from the lower end of this ramp, a long causeway ran down to the cultivation. Thanks to most careful clearance of the ground, the American Expedition found a row of holes on either side of the causeway and also that, just below the approach to the temple, there were several more of these, stretching out on either side. In many of these holes they found tree roots. So it is evident that the road leading to the temple was bordered with trees and that a green grove extended all across the temple front. It must have been a lovely sight, the white pillared temple rising above this verdure and below the towering red rocks. As to how much Mentuhotep must have spent in water to keep his trees alive—well, that was his affair.

About six hundred years after his time, and after another period of darkness and chaos had come and gone, Hatshepsut chose the same magnificent surroundings for her temple. She, too, made a causeway, which covered a considerable part of the older one, and, incidentally, preserved for us a good many of the tree roots. Her temple is much larger and is built in terraces, each of which was decorated with splendid coloured reliefs under porticoes of fluted columns. At the foot of her ramp, on either side, is a small T-shaped pool, in which some papyrus roots and a boomerang were found. The boomerang was used for catching birds, but in this tiny pool it is quite impossible there could have been any form of sport ; it must have been used in some of the many ceremonials held in this temple. It is rather better to go to Der al Bahri in the afternoon if possible, as it is in shade and the view over the sunlit valley to Luxor and Karnak when the tints of the distant hills are violet and rose is really inexpressibly beautiful.

To those who stay long enough in Luxor to cross over often and to acquire what I may call the tomb habit, the Sheikh Abd el Gurneh hill offers endless entertainment. The modern village itself is a most curious sight. All the popula-

PLATE XIII

HOUSE IN GURNEH VILLAGE

tion used to live in tombs and many still do.   Most of the daily
life goes on in a small courtyard in front, which is generally
enclosed by a brick wall and contains the children and other
live stock belonging to the family, some articles of furniture
and two or three odd mushroom-shaped mud tables raised
upon mud pedestals, which serve the double purpose of storing
grain and making sufficiently safe sleeping places for the children, out of the way of scorpions (Plate XIII).

Much has been done to rescue the painted and inscribed tombs
from the long devastation they have suffered, but when I knew
Gurneh nearly thirty years ago, the state of matters was not very
unlike what Belzoni describes it in 1817, and, though it is
really amazing that anything should have survived, it is
appalling to think how much that was beautiful and absolutely
unique, must have perished for ever.

" A traveller is generally satisfied when he has seen the
large hall, the gallery, the staircase, and as far as he can con-
veniently go : besides, he is taken up with the strange works
he observes cut in various places, and painted on each side of
the walls ; so that when he comes to a narrow and difficult
passage, or to have to descend to the bottom of a well or
cavity, he declines taking such trouble, naturally supposing
that he cannot see in these abysses any thing so magnificent
as what he sees above, and consequently deeming it useless to
proceed any farther.   Of some of these tombs many persons
could not withstand the suffocating air, which often causes
fainting.   A vast quantity of dust rises, so fine that it enters
into the throat and nostrils, and chokes the nose and mouth
to such a degree, that it requires great power of lungs to resist
it and the strong effluvia of the mummies.   This is not all ;
the entry or passage where the bodies are is roughly cut in the
rocks, and the falling of the sand from the upper part or ceiling
of the passage causes it to be nearly filled up.   In some places
there is not more than a vacancy of a foot left, which you must
contrive to pass through in a creeping posture like a snail,
on pointed and keen stones that cut like glass.   After getting
through these passages, some of them two or three hundred
yards long, you generally find a more commodious place,
perhaps high enough to sit.   But what a place of rest ! sur-

rounded by bodies, by heaps of mummies in all directions ; which, previous to my being accustomed to the sight, impressed me with horror.   The blackness of the wall, the faint light given by the candles or torches for want of air, the different objects that surrounded me, seeming to converse with each other, and the Arabs with the candles or torches in their hands, naked and covered with dust, themselves resembling living mummies, absolutely formed a scene that cannot be described.   In such a situation I found myself several times, and often returned exhausted and fainting, till at last I became inured to it, and indifferent to what I suffered, except from the dust, which never failed to choke my throat and nose ; and though fortunately, I am destitute of the sense of smelling, I could taste that the mummies were rather unpleasant to swallow.   After the exertion of entering into such a place, through a passage of fifty, a hundred, three hundred, or perhaps six hundred yards, nearly overcome, I sought a resting place, found one, and contrived to sit ; but when my weight bore on the body of an Egyptian, it crushed it like a bandbox.   I naturally had recourse to my hands to sustain my weight, but they found no better support ; so that I sunk altogether among the broken mummies, with a crash of bones, rags, and wooden cases, which raised such a dust as kept me motionless for a quarter of an hour, waiting till it subsided again.   I could not remove from the place, however, without increasing it, and every step I took I crushed a mummy in some part or other.   Once I was conducted from such a place to another resembling it, through a passage of about twenty feet in length, and no wider than that a body could be forced through.   It was choked with mummies, and I could not pass without putting my face in contact with that of some decayed Egyptian ; but as the passage inclined downwards, my own weight helped me on : however, I could not avoid being covered with bones, legs, arms, and heads rolling from above. Thus I proceeded from one cave to another, all full of mummies piled up in various ways, some standing, some lying, and some on their heads."

Belzoni goes on later :

" When I did not choose to pass the river in the night to our habitation at the temple of Luxor, I took up my lodgings in the entrance of some of the tombs along with those troglodytes. Nothing could be more amusing to me. Their dwelling is generally in the passages between the first and second entrance into a tomb. The walls and the roof are as black as any chimney. The inner door is closed up with mud, except a small aperture sufficient for a man to crawl through. Within this place the sheep are kept at night and occasionally accompany their masters in their vocal concert. Over the doorway there are always some half-broken Egyptian figures, and the two foxes, the usual guardians of burial places. A small lamp, kept alive by fat from the sheep, or rancid oil, is placed on a niche in the wall and a mat is spread on the ground ; and this formed the grand divan, wherever I was. There the people assembled round me, their conversation turning wholly on antiquities. Such a one had found such a thing, and another had discovered a tomb. Various articles were brought to sell to me, and sometimes I had reason to rejoice at having stayed there. I was sure of a supper of milk and bread served in a wooden bowl ; but whenever they supposed I should stay all night, they always killed a couple of fowls for me, which were baked in a small oven heated with pieces of Mummy cases, and sometimes with the bones and rags of the mummies themselves. It is no uncommon thing to sit down near fragments of bones ; hands, feet, or skulls are often in the way ; for these people are so accustomed to be among the mummies that they think no more of sitting on them, than on the skins of their dead calves. I also became indifferent about them at last, and would have slept in a mummy pit as readily as out of it."

Nowadays, inhabitants have all been got out of the inscribed tombs, which have been fitted with gates and are guarded by the Service des Antiquités. Moreover, they are being admirably copied by Mr. and Mrs. De Garis Davies, who have made many facsimiles in colour and beautifully accurate line drawings of several complete tombs, so there will always be a record of them.

The greater part of what is known about life in ancient Egypt comes from these tombs and they are the only source in the world for information about the Mediterranean peoples in times long before the history of other nations had begun.

There are pictures in them of Syrians, Hittites and Palestinians, painted before the Children of Israel were settled in Palestine ; of Cretans, when Crete was a great sea empire, of men from Asia Minor, Libya, Cyprus and the islands. But, naturally, there is a great deal more about the duties of officials, the houses they lived in, the taxation of the country, the Sudan trade and the greatness of Pharaoh. Gradually we begin to know what to look for. If the nobleman who owned the tomb was a high official, the king on his throne is always represented. seated on either side of the central passage ; the viceroy, if such he was, lays before him the tribute of the South, or ushers into his presence messengers bringing presents from foreign lands. If he was an irrigation inspector or a land surveyor, he paints a picture of the soil being broken up after the flood has subsided, or shows the measuring of the land under crop. Or he may tell us how he had the charge of bringing down a colossal statue or an obelisk from the granite quarries of Assuan. Indeed, there is hardly any activity of life that is not, or may not have been there. But alas ! for all that has gone. I doubt if the hundredth part remains of what was once there.

Artistically these tombs vary very much in merit. One soon gets to recognize the work of different periods, the classic, rather restrained Eighteenth Dynasty paintings, the delicate, somewhat sentimental style of Tell el Amarna and the grace-ful and flowing, if sometimes careless, lines of the Nineteenth Dynasty ; all very good when at their best.

The most celebrated of the Eighteenth Dynasty tombs is that of Rekhmara, a vizier under Thothmes III, whose tomb is a perfect mine of archæological lore. But it is difficult to see ; the light is bad and early copyists have used some varnish which has darkened the colours so much that without time and patience there is not very much to be made of it. Two or three tombs of the Tell el Amarna period are among the most beautiful in the cemetery. The tombs of Ramose and of Khaemhayt are on the low desert, between the Ramesseum and the hill of Gurneh and are hollowed out of harder and better stone than is to be found higher up. In consequence, most of the scenes have been done in relief instead of on the

flat plaster and there is, in its way, nothing more charming
in Egypt than some of the heads and figures on the walls.
The best guide to these tombs is Weigall's " Antiquities of
Upper Egypt " and a few mornings spent in rambling over the
Sheikh Abd el Gurneh, with his book in our hands, will be
reckoned among our most precious memories.

Anyone who likes walking has an advantage on excursions
like this, for the Sheikh Abd el Gurneh hill is something of
a scramble, and there are other rocky paths and valleys to
be explored where carriages and donkeys cannot follow.
Several ways lead over from Der el Bahri to the Tombs of
the Kings and though some of them are, as Baedeker would
say " only suited for experts with steady heads," any fairly
good walker can climb up by the tourist path from Der el
Bahri and follow a little footpath along the cliffs above the
temple, where the rock scenery is really extremely fine.

Another good walk is behind the Sheikh Abd el Gurneh
hill, looking into a vast amphitheatre of lofty crags. Round
it are dotted the cavernous entrances of more tombs. In
one of these, in a niche in the rock, closed up by brickwork,
the American expedition found, a few years ago, a superb
set of Middle Empire models of boats, granaries, houses, car-
pentry and cattle inspection, which have been divided between
the Museums of Cairo and of New York.

One does not realize, at first, the enormous number of
tombs there are, both on the low desert and on the hill-sides.
In the nearly precipitous cliff opposite to the American House,
a row of tombs of the Middle Empire excites our wonder as
to how the coffins were dragged up to them. Yet they were
fine tombs in their time and a recent find in one of them
is worth mention. On the very last day of what seemed a
most barren search, the American excavators found a jar full
of private letters, written on papyrus and carefully folded
and docketed. These date from about the time that Abraham
journeyed from the East into Palestine and they are extraordinarily like Egyptian letters of to-day. Mostly they are
business documents sent by an official who had gone to inspect
some land in the Delta and they have the same inordinate

amount of salaams to a very small quantity of matter, which is familiar at the present time. The letters are as yet unpublished, but I have been told of one or two which are of a more intimate nature. They were from a young woman to her mother-in-law, inquiring about " Ger " : " Why does he not write ? What is he doing ? " The docket upon them, probably in the old lady's writing, is simply " Send to Ger."

It is a mere chance to come upon so human a touch as this, but it is sad to think how much, how appallingly much more must have gone to feed the fires of the Gurneh villagers.

CHAPTER XV

LUXOR TO ASSUAN

IT is desirable to do this stretch of the river by boat, if possible, for it is difficult to see any of the temples from the train. The railway is a narrow-gauge one, slow, and the trains on it are few and so badly timed that there is just not time to go to Edfu and get back again with any comfort, for the river has to be crossed and recrossed, and the more experience one has of country ferries, the more nervous one becomes of depending on them. There is no accommodation anywhere except at Kom Ombo. It is quite possible to spend a night there on the way to or from Assuan, but, although the site of the temple is very fine, there is not much that is specially interesting about it as a building.

However, for those who cannot spare the time or the extra expense of the Nile trip, there is the consolation that Luxor and Assuan themselves are much more important than anything that lies between, and from the hot and dusty little train, one does get some idea of the different landscape that borders the river as one goes farther south.

The high red cliffs recede on the West side, soon after we leave Luxor, and, on both sides of the valley, low hills of sandstone, much strewn with boulders, come into view. At Esna, a town of some importance, the cultivation is wide for this part of Egypt and the hills are rather far away. There is a great Temple here, but most of it is still underneath the houses, as Luxor and Edfu used to be. One hall is to be seen, and is very good of its kind, but it is a Ptolemaic temple, like Edfu ; very well worth going to, if it can be seen from a boat, but hardly repaying for the long and tiring day from Luxor by train.

The chief consequence of Esna at the present day is its Barrage, subsidiary to the great one at Assuan and functioning in a different way. We have seen that the Barrage at Assiut, lower down the river, had the double use of storing a certain amount of water to irrigate the sugar- and cotton-growing lands of Middle Egypt, during the season of low Nile, and of raising the level in flood time sufficiently to fill the basins at the edge of the desert, which are not reached by the canal system. Esna, on the other hand, is only used during the inundation time, and raises the level of the water just enough to flood the Upper Egypt basins which lie between here and Assiut.

Some few miles above Esna, the character of the country changes in a marked way and becomes more like Nubia ; the cultivation shrinks to a narrow strip and sometimes disappears entirely on one side of the river, while on the other it may be a mile or less in width. The villages look much more pleasing than lower down : there are domed and barrel-vaulted roofs, and very attractive, tall, pylon-like pigeon houses, with a cornice of pots and open brick work round the top ; altogether the houses and people are cleaner and make a much more agreeable impression than the villages of Lower and Middle Egypt.

Two very ancient sites on opposite sides of the river have had much importance in history. Hieraconpolis, on the West bank, was the old capital of Upper Egypt before the First Dynasty, when Menes joined the two kingdoms and built Memphis to be the capital of the whole country. El Kab, on the East bank, was the starting-point of one of the routes to the gold mines and bears many records of this in the numbers of graffiti written and scratched on the rocks a mile or two up the Wady by which the travellers came in. Many of these rock inscriptions are primitive drawings in the style of the decorations on the prehistoric pottery and were made before writing was in use ; others are in good hieroglyphs of the Old Empire and others are later and some-what fuller. It is most curious to see the cliffs out in that lonely valley covered with these old names and records, and

it shows how we may come to bless the very practices we are
most ready to condemn—if only they are old enough ! A
pretty little Eighteenth Dynasty temple stands about a couple
of miles up the Wady ; probably it was the first point the
travellers came to from which they could see the Nile Valley
and civilization after long wanderings in search of gold.

A low hill overlooking the city enclosure is honeycombed
with tombs of a noble family who took a leading part in
freeing Egypt from the Hyksos domination. Some of these
are exceedingly interesting, and one, that of Paheri, who was
" nurse " or tutor to one of the kings, has fine work in it and
a well-known scene of the banquet, where one of the lady
guests has been overcome by the liquor she had absorbed
and some of the others make most suggestive remarks about
the thirst that consumes them. There are similar scenes in
some of the Theban tombs, so we may feel pretty confident
that drinking to excess was far from uncommon at the parties
of the period.

Paheri's is really a fine tomb, only the difficulty of getting
there is so great that it is rarely visited except from a private
steamer. The huge town wall of El Kab will be noticed by
every one who passes, either by train or boat. It is rather
mysterious why it should have been so large, for the town
seems only to have occupied a small space in one corner, but
it shows the importance the place must once have had. On
the western site, Kom el Ahmar, more anciently, Hieraconpolis, or, more anciently still, Nekhen, there is nothing at all
to be seen above ground, but in one lucky season it yielded an
extraordinary treasure of archaic objects. The old town had
been on the edge of the desert and the cultivation had never
spread over it. A few huts were dotted about on a low mound,
where my husband, who was in charge of the excavations,
believed that the temple must have been. They were unpretending dwellings, for he was able to buy out the inhabitants,
to their entire satisfaction, for ten shillings a hut. Underneath
and round about, he found, when the huts had been cleared
away, an astounding mass of relics of the earliest period of
Egyptian history, thrown away anciently, it would seem as

13

rubbish, but of priceless value as archæological material. It was probably treasure from an early temple, flung down into a cellar, perhaps because it had become old-fashioned, but possibly hidden away hurriedly to keep it out of the way of invaders. Probably both these reasons were operative, for among the " archaic " remains, there were one or two pieces of considerable intrinsic value, about a thousand years later in date, which had been buried along with them.

The sight was remarkable. Two or three trenches were filled with a miscellaneous collection of objects, all small, and mostly in bad preservation. The greater part of the mass was composed of ivory ; ivory in tusks and ivory carved into statuettes and all manner of implements.

But the condition of it was heartbreaking. For one thing it was six thousand years old, and though Kom el Ahmar is a dry spot, the damp had got into those pits and long stems of a desert plant had crept through the ivories and softened them until, as one of the party aptly said, it was like working through potted salmon. All the work, of course, was done by European hands and out of the mass of confusion we managed to rescue a quantity of figures and other small objects which held together sufficiently for it to be possible to photograph and draw them and in some cases to apply preservatives which have kept them fairly solid for five and twenty years. Naturally, if these had been found by anyone except trained observers, nothing would even have been seen there ; so there is much satisfaction in having borne even a small part in helping to save them, but it is terrible to see beautiful little statuettes—or at least statuettes which had been beautiful and are absolutely unique, perished past all recovery.

In another part lay stone mace-heads, as thick as potatoes in a pit, to use another homely simile ; these were in good enough condition, and there were also beads, stone vases, scorpions made of stone or glazed pottery, while at the bottom of the pit was found the splendid slate known as the " Hieraconpolis palette," now in Cairo Museum, and perhaps the most important monument of archaic Egypt.

Another trench produced an oddly mixed set of things.

Among them were copper statues of King Pepy I and his son, of the Sixth Dynasty. This was near the end of the Old Empire and a period when there was a great deal of traffic with the Sudan and a consequent rise in importance of all the district near the southern frontier. He almost certainly built a new temple here in the old capital and dedicated in it a new image of the Hawk god, which was the deity worshipped here. These statues are interesting artistically, as they are not of cast metal, but were made of plates beaten out and fastened on a wooden core. When found, the wooden core had long been destroyed and the plates of copper were so crumpled and broken that they were hardly recognizable as having formed parts of statues, but they have been put together with much success.

Although these were about a thousand years later in date than the bulk of the finds, they are still of the Old Empire and far the oldest life-size metal statues in existence.

But perhaps the most sensational discovery of all was in the pit which had been just underneath the altar of the temple, for in it there was found the old idol. This had been buried with care, not thrown down like the other things. The town worshipped Horus, in the form of a hawk, and the idol was a hawk of copper, with a golden head. The body, unhappily, was made, like the statues, of thin plates of metal, fixed on to wood, and the metal was so thin that it had completely corroded and fell to pieces as soon as the air from without reached it. The splendid golden head is, however, in as fine condition as the day it was made and is now a conspicuous object in the Jewel room of Cairo Museum.

The pit where it was found was dug out by a man and a boy, and great was the rejoicing and the excitement when the top of the golden feather of the Horus crown appeared. " It is a window of gold," they exclaimed, as they rushed up to give the news. For such a find, a handsome reward had to be given, and after some deliberation, it was fixed at twenty pounds, in the proportion of thirteen to the man and seven to the boy. It was not without anxiety that my husband settled on the sum, for rumours of gold had spread about rapidly and rumours of gold are generally wildly exaggerated. Would it be enough to encourage honesty yet not to pauperize the family ; above all, would public opinion consider it enough and not too much ?   Happily, it was received with enthusiasm by both parties, the man forthwith proceeding to offer his daughter in marriage to the boy, who would pay the seven pounds as dowry for her and so unite the estates.   The boy did not accept ; he alleged that the bride was too young for him and that he preferred to buy a buffalo for his family.   I never heard how they prospered after this.   It was a remote part of the country, not one from which our workmen habitually came, and we lost sight of them.

All this part of Egypt is poor enough and even round the town of Edfu the cultivation is scanty compared with the fat fields of Middle Egypt.   Edfu was at one time mostly built on the roof of the temple and visitors had to scramble down a steep slope to see the inside, but it has been entirely cleared now and is a most imposing place, for it is complete from the innermost shrine to the enclosing wall.   Certainly it is one of the greatest things to see in Egypt ; not the most beautiful, nor the most picturesque ; but nowhere else do we see so well what the temples were in their original state.   Its enormous size, the splendid building of the pylon and the lofty walls all testify to what the Ptolemaic rulers were willing to expend upon the country of their adoption.

Plate XIV gives a particularly fine idea of its stately proportions.

South of Edfu are the quarries of Silsileh, which were much worked in old times and are interesting to visit, if one gets the chance.

There are many inscriptions of different periods, one of the most curious being from the time of Seti Ist, relating what was done for the quarry workers.   Seti sent up an expedition to transport sandstone blocks for the monuments of his father Amen Ra Osiris and his " divine ennead," and this is the account of their rations.

" His Majesty, Life ! Prosperity ! Health ! increased that

PLATE XIV

TEMPLE OF EDFU

which was furnished to the army in ointment, ox-flesh, fish and plentiful vegetables without limit. Every man among them had 20 ' deben ' of bread daily, 2 bundles of vegetables, a roast of flesh ; and 2 linen garments monthly. Thus they worked with a loving heart for his Majesty, Life ! Prosperity ! Health ! " (Translation Breasted, " Records of the Past.")

Another Ptolemaic temple there is still to see before we reach Assuan ; Kom Ombo, namely, but it owes most of its beauty to its very fine situation overlooking the river. It would be tedious to enter into a detailed description of any of the temples : they are well given in Weigall's " Guide to the Antiquities of Upper Egypt."

We have noticed how the scenery altered on the way up the river from Luxor and how the more Nubian character of the landscape and the people began to show itself, but it is on arriving at Assuan that this becomes really strongly marked. Assuan is hardly to be reckoned as Egypt, for instead of the tranquilly flowing Nile that we have followed for six hundred miles, we see now a surging rapid, pouring round rocky islets out of the sun-baked south. The rosy limestone cliffs of Luxor and the drab coloured sandstone of El Kab and Silsileh have given place to the black and gold of Nubia. The granite rocks are black where the Nile washes them, and so brilliant a yellow are the sand slopes on the west that they seem to have absorbed the living sunlight.

It is one of the most fascinating places in Egypt or in the world, for the three or four months of perfect winter weather. The air is pure, the colour vivid and the views in every direction most beautiful.

Needless to say, it is not to be compared with Luxor in the way of antiquities. There is a good deal of interest at Assuan, but it was quite a different sort of place. While Luxor was a magnificent capital, Assuan was a frontier fortress, a trading post, and, especially, a quarry. That is what strikes us most. Everywhere there are inscriptions on the rocks, stating that they were made by so and so, in the reign of such and such a king, who had been sent to Assuan to fetch a fine piece of granite for a statue, a sarcophagus, a stela, or an obelisk.

He wrote all this down on some granite boulder, with suitable prayers to the local gods and, occasionally, a precious bit of biography. Inscribed stones stick up in the main street, next door to a shop which sells photographs and embroideries, others are scattered about in the public gardens, beneath private houses and round the Cataract Hotel. Sailing on the river one sees them in quantities.

Part of Assuan is known as the Bishareen camp and these queer desert Arabs, with their extraordinary heads of hair, remind us what an outpost of civilization Assuan is, with its fine hotels and clean streets. Round about it is savage desert, beyond it is tropical Africa, where the white man lives and works amid special and artificial conditions. It is the fuzzy-haired Bishareen that are here at home.

Assuan was already an important place in the Old Empire and was governed by the heads of a noble family, whose tombs are on the West bank, on the hillside surmounted by a little sheikh's tomb, known as the " Koubbet el Hawa."

These noblemen were caravan conductors to the king and had charge of the expeditions southwards to bring gold, ivory and slaves from the Sudan. The scenes in their tombs are of the regular Old Empire type, harvesting, fishing, dining ; like Sakkara, but much inferior in workmanship. One of them has, however, an extremely interesting inscription, much quoted, to the effect that Herkhuf, the owner of the tomb, had made four journeys to the land of " Yam " ; that, on the fourth occasion he had been able to secure a dancing dwarf from the land of the pygmies, which he was sending to the king. King Pepy II, then a boy, was so delighted with the prospect of the dwarf that he wrote back to Herkhuf to enjoin him to

" Come northward to the Court immediately ; thou shalt bring this dwarf with thee, which thou bringest living, prosperous and healthy from the land of spirits, for the dances of the god, to rejoice and gladden the heart of the King. . . . When he goes down with thee into the vessel appoint excellent people, who shall be beside him on each side of the vessel ; take care lest he fall into the water. When he sleeps at night appoint excellent people, who shall sleep beside him in his tent ; inspect ten times a night. My majesty desires to see this dwarf more than the gifts of Sinai and Punt." (Mrans. Breasted.)

This family lasted on until the Middle Empire, and of that period there is a very fine tomb, the outer hall undecorated, but beautifully hewn out of the hard rock and giving a vista between the columns and along a corridor, to a brilliantly coloured stela at the end, where Serenput, the owner, sits at his meal.

A possible addition to this excursion to the tombs is to the Monastery of St. Simeon, but some people will prefer to make it the object of a special trip, for though there are not many who are interested in Christian architecture, it is a curious place to see and commands very fine views of the valley. The sail across the Nile is always delightful and the climb up to the ruins is short and easy, unless in very hot weather. The little Monastery was never one of the great sanctuaries of Egypt, but it is comparatively well preserved and we can understand how the old hermit after whom it is named, must have established himself first in an old tomb or cavern, around which, as his holiness became celebrated throughout the land, other anchorites gathered themselves into a community and built the church, cells, refectory and all the other necessary buildings. They may have utilized the remains of an old Roman fortress, for indeed they required walls of defence against the attacks of desert tribes. There is wild, savage-looking desert out to the west, over the yellow sands, but to the north and south, the windings of the blue river, fringed by a narrow strip of verdure and dotted with numberless islands, are very lovely.

As we return, we round the southern point of Elephantine, once crowned with temples like Philæ, but now a depressing heap of brick ruins. Even as late as 1822 a temple of the Eighteenth Dynasty was standing there, but Mehemet Aly wanted to have a palace at Assuan, and in order to build it, destroyed the temple, broke up the granite for building material and burnt the limestone to make the mortar. Since then a great part of the remaining mound has been carried away by the " sebakhin "—the peasants carting manure, to whom we have had so often to refer—but in spite of all this, it has been worth while to dig there and valuable antiquities have been discovered among this unpromising-looking rubbish.

Assuan was specially devoted to the worship of the god Khnum, in the form of a ram, and some visitors to Cairo Museum may have been struck by large mummified rams covered with gold foil, which were found on Elephantine. More important, however, were two finds of papyri, one in very ancient Egyptian, the other dating from about 450 B.C., when a colony of Jews was settled at Assuan. It was probably a military colony, placed there by the Persians, who were in possession of Egypt at that time. The papyri are written in Aramaic and have thrown light upon many linguistic questions, but their chief interest is the surprising fact that they reveal the existence of a temple to Jehovah on the island of Elephantine, just about the time that Ezra and Nehemiah were rebuilding the temple at Jerusalem and actually mentioning some of the names of officials which occur in their writings.

A small red-roofed house on the island, once an irrigation rest house, now contains most of the antiquities found in the course of the excavations in Nubia which were carried out by the Egyptian Government, in view of the raising of the Assuan dam to a level which would flood a large area to the south. The collection is well labelled and arranged and is very interesting, especially as regards the prehistoric objects ; all the well-known Egyptian types being found in Nubia just a little later.

But the great charm of Assuan is just—Assuan ; the river, the great black rocks rising out of the water, like giant elephants bathing, the golden desert, the vivid green of the trees. Generally speaking, sailing in a small boat on the Nile is not particularly inviting, but here at Assuan nothing could be more attractive. A charming spot for a picnic is Sehel, an island to the south of Assuan, just below the Cataract. It was the old frontier of Egypt proper and the south end of the island is literally covered with inscriptions on every face of the tumbled granite crags. The boat lands us on the east bank of the island, and quite near, but a little to the south, are two or three rather important graffiti relating to a canal which was made in the Middle Empire, but fell out of use, became blocked and was cleared again by Thothmes I. One or two of these inscriptions are very well and clearly written and so easy to translate that they are usually the first piece of hieroglyphic that is given to a beginners' class. The purport is :

" Year 3, first month of the third season, under the majesty of king Aa Kheper Ka Ra (Thothmes I.) who is given life. His majesty commanded to dig this canal, after he found it stopped up with stones, so that no ship sailed upon it. He sailed down stream upon it, his heart glad, having slain his enemies."

But the more exciting part of the island lies some little way off. On a high outcrop of rock near the southern end, almost every stone has figures or hieroglyphs cut on it, even on the most inaccessible-looking pinnacles. It is a most curious and entertaining sight even for those who are unable to decipher any of them. Most are amazingly clearly cut and the figures are drawn with a fine, bold line. In this wonderful climate they have lasted with little damage for three thousand years and more, and, if some slight knowledge of the old language enables us to pick out records and prayers written by the very men whose tombs we have seen on the Sheikh Abd el Gurneh hill at Thebes, where we have read of their expeditions to Assuan and Nubia, it feels like meeting with old friends and gives us the rare human touch which means so much in the dreary waste of Egyptian annals.

Other characteristic sights of Assuan are the old quarries. The most famous object there, an unfinished obelisk, is not far from the town, just beyond the Arab cemetery. It is larger than any of the obelisks now standing and it was found to be too much flawed to be possible to remove it. Another attempt was made to cut it down to a smaller size, but again the granite was not of good enough quality right through and the whole thing was abandoned and lies as it was left there, sometime in the Eighteenth Dynasty.

To the unmechanical, feminine mind, it is a tremendous help to see such a thing, and makes it far easier to realize the vastness of the undertaking it was to hew out that obelisk, to haul it to the river bank, transport it to Luxor and set it up within the temple walls. I am glad to find that point of view recognized in Mr. Engelbach's interesting and exhaustive book " The Problem of the Obelisk," to which readers are referred for a full account of how the ancient Egyptians carried out the job, the tools they used and the amount of time and labour that they employed.

In another quarry, much nearer Shellal, there are one or two other unfinished pieces which are worth seeing. Two large sarcophagi, " baths " as the Arabs call them, have been left half hollowed out on the hillside, and a colossal figure, perhaps the lid of a stone coffin, lies partly buried in the sand. None of these were very promising as regards workmanship, and are really much more impressive in the quarry than they would have been if they had been finished, but one fine Eighteenth Dynasty inscription on a rock near by is as good and clear cut as if it had been done yesterday. All is as it was, and the desert here must look just as it did long ago, except for the gangs of workmen that were busy working with their stone tools and hauling the mighty blocks over the sands to the river. The landscape is so unchanged and unchanging that our mind readily turns to picture the past as we walk down the sandy slope from the quarries, but gets pulled back to the present—indeed to the future—with a sudden jerk, when, down on the flat plain before us, we see an aerodrome, where the planes flying to or from Khartoum alight and spend a night.

CHAPTER XVI

ASSUAN TO ABU SIMBEL

IN the old days it was part of the recognized programme for a dahabieh to be hauled up the cataract by sheer man power, but, as a large boat was difficult to manage, parties often had to hire what they could find at Assuan to take them up to the higher stretches of the river. Shellal, at the top of the cataract, is now the terminus of the railway from Cairo, so travellers going to the Sudan alight there and go straight on board the Sudan Government steamer. There are also tourist boats belonging to Cook and to the Anglo-American Nile Co., which arrange a delightful week's trip to Wady Halfa and back, giving time to visit all the temples on the way. It is a most fascinating bit of the river. The dreamy, peaceful days of blue water, black rocks and golden sands, ruins of ancient towns and temples succeed each other in a heavenly monotony. It is true that none of the temples, except Abu Simbel, is of the first importance ; hardly, indeed, of the second, but the charm of the whole scenery is unsurpassed.

Those who cannot afford time for this extra week on the Nile, can get some idea of the Nubian landscape by going up for a day to Philæ from Assuan. But it is only in the early winter that much of Philæ is out of water. The great dam is best visited from Assuan, and is a very imposing sight. As is well remembered, much controversy raged around the making of it ; beauty and utility, agriculture and archæology were set in opposing camps, and it was only after every other possible place had been considered that it was agreed on that the advantages of Assuan were so great that they outweighed the drawbacks.

But after the present site had been selected, there were still many difficulties to be surmounted. The first years, when the foundations were being dug and the masonry built up to the water-level, were full of anxiety. The foundations had to be dug deeper than had been estimated, for though the stone below the river-bed was all granite, the upper layers of it were cracked and fissured by the violence of the stream, and the vast mass of masonry that was to be built could not rest on anything but the living rock. In one part the blasting out of this inferior stone went down to fifteen metres before the unflawed granite was reached. Meanwhile the great volume of the Nile flood could not be diverted from its channel; at most the channel could be a little narrowed. Out from either side an embankment was thrown, above and below the line where the dam was to be; the ends met upon one of the rocky islets in the stream, equidistant from the shore on both sides; thus forming two large tanks or basins, and driving the current of the river down the middle. The water was then pumped out of these tanks and the rock left bare for the excavations to begin. The foundations were laid, the great wall of masonry built, complete with all its sluices. Then the temporary dykes were removed and the water allowed to pour through the sluices. And so, from island to island, pushing out from side to side, the process was repeated; all the stream passing through the sluices at the side while the centre part was being excavated.

The first dam was completed in 1902, but not the dam originally contemplated, which was designed to be much higher and to have greatly more storage capacity. But the scheme had aroused such serious opposition owing to the inevitable submergence of Philæ, that the plan had been modified. The reservoir was first used in 1903, and very soon after that, the engineers became alarmed at the enormous blocks of granite that were being dislodged by the thundering waters. For the second time the rocky bottom had to be uncovered and the deep holes which had been scoured out filled with masonry, making a sort of granite apron, which sloped gradually up to the sluice gates. This has been perfectly satisfactory, but the work was not at an end.

The benefits of the increased water were so great that demands for the fullest possible supply became more and more urgent and the Egyptian Government finally decided that the claims of art and archæology must be disregarded in favour of the pressing needs of the present : in other words, that the dam must be raised to the level originally designed and Philæ must be sacrificed.

Everything that could be done was done to preserve it and the other temples of Nubia.   Very large sums were spent on the underpinning of the foundations of Philæ, some of which were resting on Nile mud and would have been very short-lived, while, thanks to the work carried out, the ruins are, so far, very little the worse for their annual immersion. Besides the money spent on the temples, the Government had to pay compensation to the proprietors of land and houses in the area that was about to be flooded and to rebuild the villages above the water line ; no light matter, when we reflect that the effect of the heading back of the water is felt for nearly two hundred miles to the south.   A grant was given for excavating the ancient cemeteries that were to be affected by the reservoir and the results of this digging were fully published by the Survey Department.

The raising of the dam was, naturally, much more of a problem than it would have been to have built it all to the original design.   Once again, the bed of the river had to be laid bare bit by bit, and the rock blasted out to make foundations.   Then a curious difficulty confronted the engineers. I quote from the Public Works report :

" Masonry, when built under the fierce tropical heat which prevails at Assuan, absorbs a considerable quantity of this heat.   This, with the lapse of time, gradually vanishes away and the building cools down internally to a more or less fixed temperature : the result of this cooling making itself apparent in cracks which usually occur at fairly regular intervals in all masonry structures.   The outer layer of masonry, as well as the lower internal mass, also experience this change of temperature, but in their case it is complicated by the annual climatic change in the surrounding air, with the result that these cracks, which are visible in winter, close again almost completely in the summer. There is thus an annual expansion and contraction of the outer layers, at least, of the structure. A new mass of masonry placed against an older building would not respond in the same manner to temperature changes until it had itself reached internally the same condition as the building against which it was placed. Sir Benjamin Baker, in considering this problem, suggested that the best method of overcoming the difficulty would be to leave a space between the two walls of from 2 to 6 inches ; this space to be eventually filled up with liquid cement when the new wall reached the same phase of temperature condition as the old. This it was estimated would occur after the lapse of not less than two years."

This proceeding was carried out with complete success and the engineering details of it are interesting even to the non-technical visitors.

The dam was completed in 1912, was first utilized in the following year, and in 1914, when the Nile flood was the lowest on record, there is no doubt that it saved the country from famine.

The Barrage begins to function after the flood has subsided. From July to mid-November, or even later, the sluices are all open, so that the silt-bearing water flows through, as if the dam were not there. When the flood is over and the water clear of silt, a few of the gates are shut and the level of the reservoir gradually raised until about the middle of March, when the dammed-up water reaches the height we can see traced by a white line on Philæ temple, on the surrounding islands and on the shore. After the end of March, when Egypt is in need of the summer water supply, as many sluices are opened as are required to keep the river up to its spring level. By July the reservoir is empty and the first swelling of the next year's flood begins to make itself felt. Incidentally, the discharge from one of the sluices is measured into a tank, thus forming an extremely accurate Nile gauge, so that practically every gallon of water that the giant river pours

PLATE XV.

PHILÆ FROM WEST

down is calculated and the prospects for the irrigation of the
country regulated with great exactness.

Turning now from the romance of modern science to look
at the jewel of the old world that has had to make way for it,
we must realize, even seeing Philæ at the best of times, that
much of its beauty has perished. I never saw it before the
dam was made, but the temple and its setting have been written
of in such terms that we cannot fail to feel that it must have
been one of the most lovely spots in Egypt.

If one is fortunate enough to be there early in the season,
Philæ is still to be seen, in a sense, as well as ever, for the
damage done by the water is astonishingly slight and the
sculptures are still crisp and clear upon walls and columns
that have had their annual drenching for years past. But
the picturesqueness of the place must have depended more
on the Coptic village that clung about the skirts of the
temple, the palm trees that surrounded it and the groves that
fringed the river banks. Now all that has vanished and the
ruins stand stark and bare on their island, while the shores
on both sides of the Nile are desolate and uninhabited. All
the villages which used to border the river have been removed
and rebuilt above the straight white line which is left by the
highest level of the water in the reservoir (Plate XV). This
photograph was taken some years ago, when a few palm trees
were still surviving. It is from the Island of Biggeh. But it
is still a beautiful place, a great gateway, as it were, to the
tropical Africa to which we are drawing near. The scenery
is in striking contrast to Egypt. The sands are more golden,
the air is clearer, the tumbled black rocks of Biggeh and the
southern desert look savage and unfinished, as if Nature, in
some far-off age, had thrown them down and forgotten them.
I suppose, in summer, the heat is fiercer, but as I write these
lines on the roof of Philæ temple, on a November morning,
the breeze is so cool that it is hard to realize it.

Now, in November, we can walk everywhere ; in fact, the
temple floor is high above water-level and round about, on
the river's brink, there is just a faint little edging of green,
a scanty bean crop that may be gathered before the water

rises, and a little grassy browsing for the goats. Later, in
January perhaps, some of the temple can be seen by boat,
but in February and March, only the very highest parts
rise above the water. As we see it, in the early winter, it
is a very impressive place. So, indeed, are all these Ptolemaic
temples, however much we may profess to look down on the
art they contain.

The reliefs are ugly ? Yes, no doubt, but look at the one
little bit of roof in the Isis temple, just above the water-level,
where the colour has survived time and the flood, and think
what it must all have been like once. I do not believe that
the round, fat work would have made much difference to
the beauty of the decoration as seen from a distance. And
Philæ, rising from the midst of the blue waters and the rugged
crags, with its gaily coloured walls and brilliant flags flying
above the pylons, must have looked superb, and must have
gladdened the eyes of many a wanderer coming back from
the barbaric, tropical Sudan, with the first sight of the gorgeous
and civilized land of Egypt.

It was not there in the greatest days of Egypt ; it is one of
the latest in date of all the temples and the one where the
old religion lingered longest after Christianity was established
in the rest of the country. From the archæological point of
view, it was probably one that could be spared as well as
any, and when we see the extraordinary prosperity to which
Egypt has attained since the construction of the dam and the
increased population she is now able to support in comparative
well-being, it can scarcely be questioned that it was right to
put the interests of the present before the claims of antiquity ;
prosperity before æsthetics. Yet in some of us a rebellious
voice still murmurs, asking whether it might not have been
as well for the world to have kept the rushing cataract un-
impeded and Philæ with its palms—even if there had not
been quite so many Egyptians.

On Biggeh Island there is a temple, too, just opposite to
Philæ, but not much of it remains. The graffiti on the island
are interesting and there are many of them, some as old
as the Eighteenth Dynasty and of good work. It is worth

a little scramble to see them, if one is active and sufficiently interested.

Going southwards up the river, as the stern-wheeler churns its way into Lower Nubia, our feeling of remoteness from the world grows ever stronger, for now at last the railway is left behind, posts are rare, and life flows peacefully by on the tranquil waters.

The two days on the steamer make a pleasant break in the long journey to Khartoum and a stop is usually made at Abu Simbel, long enough to get some idea of the place, but apart from it the Sudan passengers do not see any of the other temples, and, though none but Abu Simbel is of the first importance, there is a good deal that is worth seeing, and the comfortable, leisurely trip from Shellal to Halfa by the tourist boat is a delightful experience.

A good deal depends upon the season as to how much of the temples can be seen, as after December, when the reservoir is beginning to fill, some of the ruins are either totally or partially submerged. But the best are, fortunately, above the high-water level, and there are so many of them, that to most people a Ptolemaic temple or so, more or less, cannot be said to make much difference.

The scenery is fine ; in some parts might be called magnificent, such as the Babel Kalabsheh, where the Nile pours through a narrow channel between precipitous hills. If one climbs up to the high desert, from almost any point there are grand views over the singularly savage and desolate Nubian desert and the Nile, with scarcely a strip of verdure on its banks. Lower Nubia must always have been poor and barren, yet from very early times it was of importance to Egypt because of the trade from the Sudan, so it had to be strongly held and the Bedouin tribes that wandered about it kept in order. So long ago as the Old Empire, we have seen that expeditions were sent up, partly trading, partly military. Almost throughout history these Lower Nubian people kept loyal to Egypt, but they sometimes had to be defended against their warlike neighbours to the south and the frontier tended always to be pushed farther up the Nile. By the Middle

14

Empire it was at Semneh above the Second Cataract, and at that time no negroes were allowed to come north of the fortresses there, unless provided with a permit for trading.

Still farther off, in Dongola province, Dr. Reisner found the grave of an Egyptian governor of that period, a native of Assiut, who had prepared a fine tomb for himself in the cemetery of his native town. But instead of being buried there, at home, with the familiar, civilized rites of Egyptian burial, he died at his distant post and was laid to rest there, like a savage chieftain, surrounded by troops of slaves who were slaughtered to bear him company into the unknown. In the New Empire the traffic with the Sudan became more and more important. The tombs at Luxor are full of pictures of the gold and ivory and other products of the tropics that were brought to the capital, and among the titles of several of the highest noblemen or members of the Royal family who are buried there was that of " Viceroy of Kush."

A curious political change took place some centuries later, about the time of the Kings of Israel and Judah. The whole of Nubia had, long before that time, been permeated with Egyptian customs and culture. Some dispossessed Egyptian rulers had fled to the Sudan and established themselves there, and from their admixture with a vigorous southern people there arose an exceedingly powerful race of kings, who for a time ruled over the whole of Egypt down to the sea, and who met the brunt of the Assyrian invasion. In Second Kings, we read of Tirhaka, King of Ethiopia, coming against the Assyrian army in Palestine ; and, if we happen to think of it, it is rather surprising to hear that Ethiopia should have had any concern with the advance of the Assyrians. But it was just at this time, when Tirhaka (Taharka) was actually over-lord of Egypt, that this advance occurred and Tirhaka came all the way down the Nile to protect his dominions from invasion. He did temporarily throw his assailants back out of Egypt and returned to his capital at Meroe, in Dongola province, where the pyramid in which he was buried has lately been discovered.

The Assyrians came back, however, in the reign of his

son, and conquered the whole of Egypt up to Thebes. For some centuries after that time the two kingdoms of Egypt and Nubia have a separate history, but Lower Nubia became subject to Egypt once more and was strongly garrisoned in Ptolemaic and Roman times. Christianity seems to have been established pretty early, but after the Roman troops were withdrawn, the history is very obscure. When there no longer was a strong power either to the north or the south, this barren stretch of country inevitably relapsed into its natural poverty and the few glimpses we have of it show a condition of barbarism and misery. Belzoni was up there a good deal, as he did a certain amount of digging at Abu Simbel and he found the people most difficult to work with. They had never seen money and literally did not know what they were to do with it ; they were all nearly in a state of famine and they were most unwilling to labour at anything which required steady effort. Turkish officials there were, of a low class, who mulcted the unhappy peasants of everything that could be taken off them. Altogether a gloomy picture.

At the present day, I should think they are well off ; not that the country can be made to produce more, but the inhabitants have found an occupation at which they are surprisingly good ; that of domestic service. A great number of the best cooks and sofragis in Cairo have their homes in the clean little villages that we pass between Assuan and Halfa. It is a clean country ; that is one of the pleasant things about this journey, and the villages are very attractive.

The temples are of various dates ; there is nothing in the way of regular building earlier than the New Empire, but there are plenty of rock inscriptions to show where the earlier expeditions halted and what their objects had been. The temples, forts and town sites grow confused in one's recollection after much time has passed, for there is not much that is of the highest class of art, but the wonderful succession of fine buildings that rise out of a country so wild and desolate, is a strange and fascinating sight.

The most beautiful part of the journey is perhaps the few miles between Philæ and Kalabsheh, where the small

14*

temple of Bet el Waly, on the hillside above the big Kalabsheh temple, contains really fine and interesting scenes of the campaigns of Rameses II against the Ethiopians, and the lists of tribute he exacted from them.

Just beyond Kalabsheh we enter the tropics, and some travellers would have it that the cool breeze of evening is less felt after this point, but that is hardly likely. At Kasr Ibrim, a frowning fortress on the east bank, the view from the height is well worth the climb up to it. Nowhere is the impression of savage nature more violently borne in upon us than from this gloomy outpost. Strange scenes must have taken place within its walls. It was first an old Egyptian fort, then a Roman frontier station—surely one of the most remote of the far-flung empire—then, long after, when the Turks had conquered Egypt early in the sixteenth century, the Sultan Selim placed a Bosnian garrison there, and forgot it! There these soldiers hung on, a Christian, semi-civilized colony, until the Mamelukes, retreating into the Sudan, after Mehemet Aly's massacre of their more distinguished brethren, captured the place and turned out the Bosnians, or rather those of the descendants of the Bosnians who still inhabited the fort, for the two or three centuries the Bosnian occupation lasted seem to have perceptibly lightened the complexions of the villagers for some distance round.

More and more temples and ruins of towns succeed one another all the way until the last and greatest is reached. So much has been written about Abu Simbel that one hardly dares to hope that it will come up to what we have imagined. But it does, and more. It ranks among the very great things of Egypt and has, besides, the glamour of its remoteness and the strange beauty of the lonely miles of river that we have traversed to reach it. Often, down in Egypt, we have been disposed to look on the work of Rameses II as showy and ostentatious, to condemn him for unscrupulously using the work of better men than himself and calling it his own ; in short, to consider him as the beginning of the decadence. But at Abu Simbel, all such criticism is silenced. Here, on the utmost confines of his Empire, in the desolate, sun-steeped desert, is the last of the Egyptian temples and one of the grandest. A few words from abler pens than mine will tell of the memory it leaves.

Miss Martineau thus describes her first sight of it :

" The seriousness I plead for comes of itself into the mind of any thoughtful and feeling traveller at such a moment as that of entering the great temple of Abu Simbel, I entered it at an advantageous moment when the morning sunshine was reflected from the sand outside, so as to cast a twilight even into the adytum,—two hundred feet from the entrance. The four tall statues in the adytum, ranged behind the altar, were dimly visible : and I hastened to them, past the eight Osirides, through the next pillared hall, and across the corridor. And then I looked back, and saw beyond the dark halls and shadowy Osirides, the golden sand hill without, a corner of blue sky and a gay group of the crew in the sunshine. It was like looking out upon life from the grave."

Miss Amelia B. Edwards, whose artistic appreciations are often very valuable, spent nearly three weeks at Abu Simbel and tells of it in one of the best passages of her " Thousand Miles up the Nile."

" Stupendous as they are, nothing is more difficult than to see the colossi properly. Standing between the rock and the river, one is too near ; stationed on the island opposite, one is too far off ; while from the sand slope only a side view is obtainable. Hence, for want of a fitting standpoint, many travellers have seen nothing but deformity in the most perfect face handed down to us by Egyptian art.

" The profile of the southernmost colossus can be correctly seen from but one point of view ; and that point is where the sand slope meets the northern buttress of the façade, at a level just parallel with the beards of the statues. The sand slope is steep, and loose, and hot to the feet. More disagreeable climbing it would be hard to find, even in Nubia, but no traveller who refuses to encounter this small hardship need believe that he has seen the faces of the colossi. Viewed from below, the face is shortened out of all proportion. It looks unduly wide from ear to ear, while the lips and the lower part

of the nose show relatively larger than the rest of the features.
The same may be said of the great cast in the British Museum.

" The artists who wrought the original statues, however,
were embarrassed by no difficulties of focus, daunted by no
difficulties of scale.   Giants themselves, they summoned these
giants from the solid rock and endowed them with superhuman
strength and beauty.   They sought no quarried blocks of
syenite or granite for their work.   They fashioned no models
of clay.   They took a mountain and fell upon it like Titans,
and hollowed it and carved it as though it were a cherry stone
and left it for the feebler men of after ages to marvel at for
ever.   One great hall and fifteen spacious chambers they
hewed out from the heart of it ; then smoothed the rugged
precipice towards the river,' and cut four huge statues with
their faces to the sunrise, two to the right and two to the left
of the doorway, there to keep watch to the end of time."

INDEX

Printed in Great Britain by
Butler & Tanner Ltd.,
Frome and London